The First Letter to the Corinthians

OneBook.
DAILY-WEEKLY

The First Letter to the Corinthians

T. Michael W. Halcomb

Copyright 2023 by T. Michael W. Halcomb

All rights reserved. No part of this publication may be reproduced, stored in a retrieval system, or transmitted, in any form or by any means—electronic, mechanical, photocopying, recording, or otherwise—without prior written permission, except for brief quotations in critical reviews or articles.

Scripture quotations are taken from the Holy Bible, New International Version®, NIV® Copyright © 1973, 1978, 1984, 2011 by Biblica, Inc.® Used by permission of Zondervan. All rights reserved worldwide. www.zondervan.com The "NIV" and "New International Version" are trademarks registered in the United States Patent and Trademark Office by Biblica, Inc.™ All rights reserved worldwide.

Scripture quotations marked CEB are from the COMMON ENGLISH BIBLE © Copyright 2011 COMMON ENGLISH BIBLE. All rights reserved. Used by permission. (www.CommonEnglishBible.com).

Scripture quotations marked ESV are from the ESV® Bible (The Holy Bible, English Standard Version®), copyright © 2001 by Crossway, a publishing ministry of Good News Publishers. Used by permission. All rights reserved.

Scripture quotations marked NABRE are taken from the *New American Bible, revised edition*© 2010, 1991, 1986, 1970 Confraternity of Christian Doctrine, Washington, D.C. and are used by permission of the copyright owner. All Rights Reserved. No part of the New American Bible may be reproduced in any form without permission in writing from the copyright owner.

The Scriptures marked NET are from the NET Bible® http://netbible.com copyright ©1996, 2019 used with permission from Biblical Studies Press, L.L.C. All rights reserved.

Scripture quotations marked NLT are taken from the Holy Bible, New Living Translation, copyright © 1996, 2004, 2015 by Tyndale House Foundation. Used by permission of Tyndale House Publishers, Inc., Carol Stream, Illinois 60188. All rights reserved.

Scripture quotations marked NRSV are taken from New Revised Standard Version Bible, copyright © 1989 National Council of the Churches of Christ in the United States of America. Used by permission. All rights reserved.

Scripture quotations marked (NIrV) are taken from the Holy Bible, New International Reader's Version®, NIrV® Copyright © 1995, 1996, 1998, 2014 by Biblica, Inc.™ Used by permission of Zondervan. All rights reserved worldwide. www.zondervan.com The "NIrV" and "New International Reader's Version" are trademarks registered in the United States Patent and Trademark Office by Biblica, Inc.™

Scripture quotations marked CSB have been taken from the Christian Standard Bible®, Copyright © 2017 by Holman Bible Publishers. Used by permission. Christian Standard Bible® and CSB® are federally registered trademarks of Holman Bible Publishers.

Printed in the United States of America

Cover design by Strange Last Name
Page design and layout by PerfecType, Nashville, Tennessee

Halcomb, T. Michael W.
 The first letter to the Corinthians / T. Michael W. Halcomb. – Franklin, Tennessee : Seedbed Publishing, ©2023.

pages ; cm. + 1 video disc. – (OneBook. Daily-weekly)

Includes bibliographical references.
ISBN: 9781628249392 (paperback)
ISBN: 9781628249439 (DVD)
ISBN: 9781628249408 (mobi)
ISBN: 9781628249415 (epub)
ISBN: 9781628249422 (pdf)
OCLC: 1372341994

1. Bible. Corinthians, 1st --Textbooks. 2. Bible. Corinthians, 1st--Study and teaching. 3. Bible. Corinthians, 1st--Commentaries. I. Title. II. Series.

BV2675.55.H34 2023   227/.2   2023934539

SEEDBED PUBLISHING
Franklin, Tennessee

CONTENTS

Welcome to OneBook Daily-Weekly — ix

Week One
Dear Corinth . . . — 1
1 Corinthians 1:1–25

Day One: Better Call Paul — 2
Day Two: Thank God — 4
Day Three: United Way — 6
Day Four: Troublin' the Waters — 7
Day Five: Four Big Buts — 9
Week One Gathering Discussion Outline — 12

Week Two
No Cracks in the Foundation — 14
1 Corinthians 1:26–3:32

Day One: *Ones* upon a Time — 14
Day Two: Rulers Not Measuring Up — 16
Day Three: Reality Check — 18
Day Four: Growing Pains — 20
Day Five: Made in Corinth — 22
Week Two Gathering Discussion Outline — 25

Week Three
Paul's Apology — 27
1 Corinthians 4:1–21

Day One: Can't Judge This — 28
Day Two: Starting to Reign — 30

Day Three: Processing the Procession ... 32
Day Four: Like Father, like Son ... 34
Day Five: Coming Soon ... 36
Week Three Gathering Discussion Outline ... 38

Week Four
Incest, Sex, and Church Discipline ... 40
1 Corinthians 5:1–13

Day One: The Trading Bunch ... 41
Day Two: Over and Out ... 43
Day Three: Out with the Old, in with the New ... 45
Day Four: Guilty by Association ... 46
Day Five: It's What's on the Inside ... 48
Week Four Gathering Discussion Outline ... 51

Week Five
Judges, Swindlers, and the Sexually Immoral ... 53
1 Corinthians 6:1–20

Day One: Been There, Done That! ... 54
Day Two: Family Feud ... 56
Day Three: A Good Heir Day ... 58
Day Four: The Body Politic ... 60
Day Five: Best Buy ... 62
Week Five Gathering Discussion Outline ... 64

Week Six
Love and Marriage ... 66
1 Corinthians 7:1–40

Day One: Come Together ... 67
Day Two: Let It Be ... 69
Day Three: Situation Ethics? ... 71
Day Four: A Spouse Divided ... 73

Contents

Day Five: Virgin Ground — 76
Week Six Gathering Discussion Outline — 78

Week Seven
Paul's Slave-of-Christ Ethic — 80
1 Corinthians 8:1–9:27

Day One: Table Talk — 81
Day Two: The Meat of the Matter — 83
Day Three: Patron(izing) — 86
Day Four: Relinquishing Rights — 88
Day Five: Freely Give — 90
Week Seven Gathering Discussion Outline — 92

Week Eight
More on Food and Idols — 94
1 Corinthians 10:1–11:1

Day One: Can I Get a Witness? — 95
Day Two: The Temptations — 96
Day Three: Bread Ties — 98
Day Four: Foods with Benefits — 100
Day Five: Conscientious Objectors — 102
Week Eight Gathering Discussion Outline — 105

Week Nine
Head Coverings, Meals, Spiritual Gifts, and More — 107
1 Corinthians 11:2–12:31

Day One: Over Her Head — 107
Day Two: Food Fights — 110
Day Three: A Drink Called Judgment — 112
Day Four: Gift Return — 114
Day Five: Bodybuilding — 116
Week Nine Gathering Discussion Outline — 119

Week Ten
Love and Edification   121
1 Corinthians 13:1–14:19

Day One: What's Love Got to Do with It?	122
Day Two: Mirror, Mirror	124
Day Three: Profiting from Prophecy	126
Day Four: The Sound Barrier	128
Day Five: Tongue Twister	130
Week Ten Gathering Discussion Outline	133

Week Eleven
The Church: Her People, Her Gifts, and Her Gospel   135
1 Corinthians 14:20–15:11

Day One: Are You out of Your Mind?	135
Day Two: Three's Company	137
Day Three: Submissive Misses or Missing the Point?	139
Day Four: Ifs, Ands, and Buts	141
Day Five: Hold on Tight	143
Week Eleven Gathering Discussion Outline	146

Week Twelve
The Lord, the Apostles, and All the Brothers and Sisters in Christ   148
1 Corinthians 15:12–16:24

Day One: Dead or Alive	149
Day Two: The Walking Dead	151
Day Three: Resurrection	153
Day Four: Open-Door Policy	156
Day Five: A Travelin' Band	158
Week Twelve Gathering Discussion Outline	160

WELCOME TO ONEBOOK DAILY-WEEKLY

John Wesley, in a letter to one of his leaders, penned the following:

> O begin! Fix some part of every day for private exercises. You may acquire the taste which you have not: what is tedious at first, will afterwards be pleasant. Whether you like it or not, read and pray daily. It is for your life; there is no other way; else you will be a trifler all your days. . . . Do justice to your own soul; give it time and means to grow. Do not starve yourself any longer. Take up your cross and be a Christian altogether.

Rarely are our lives most shaped by our biggest ambitions and highest aspirations. Rather, our lives are most shaped, for better or for worse, by those small things we do every single day.

At Seedbed, our biggest ambition and highest aspiration is to resource the followers of Jesus to become lovers and doers of the Word of God every single day, to become people of One Book.

To that end, we have created the OneBook Daily-Weekly. First, it's important to understand what this is not: warm, fuzzy, sentimental devotions. If you engage the Daily-Weekly for any length of time, you will learn the Word of God, you will grow profoundly in your love for God, and you will become a passionate lover of people.

How Does the Daily-Weekly Work?

Daily. As the name implies, every day invites a short but substantive engagement with the Bible. Five days a week you will read a passage of Scripture followed by a short segment of teaching and closing with questions for reflection and self-examination. On the sixth day, you will review and reflect on the previous five days.

Weekly. Each week, on the seventh day, find a way to gather with at least one other person doing the study. Pursue the weekly guidance for gathering. Share learning, insight, encouragement, and most important, how the Holy Spirit is working in your lives.

That's it. Depending on the length of the study, when the eight or twelve weeks are done, we will be ready with the next study. On an ongoing basis, we will release new editions of the Daily-Weekly. Over time, those who pursue this course of learning will develop a rich library of Bible learning resources for the long haul.

OneBook Daily-Weekly will develop eight- and twelve-week studies that cover the entire Old and New Testaments. Seedbed will publish new studies regularly so that an ongoing supply of group lessons will be available. All titles will remain accessible, which means they can be used in any order that fits your needs or the needs of your group.

If you are looking for a substantive study to learn Scripture through a steadfast method, look no further.

WEEK ONE

1 Corinthians 1:1–25

Dear Corinth . . .

INTRODUCTION

If First Corinthians were a show, it might be slotted into the daytime-talk genre alongside Maury Povich or Jerry Springer. Or, better yet, it might fit well within the *Real Housewives* genre. First Corinthians has it all: fighting, sex, jealousy, divorce, money, death, and even a tryst between a stepson and stepmom. Some in the Corinthian congregation seemed to be high-fiving about such things! This letter is fifty shades of crazy!

Like many of the apostle's letters, this one reminds us how messed up the early church was. In some ways, that's good news. Two thousand years on, the church is still messed up. The difference is that we have the opportunity to learn from their epic fails. But it's sad news too. Things are being celebrated within the church today, sinful things, which the founders of our faith ardently opposed. Thus, we're left to wonder: *Can this epistle offer some guidance on such things?* I believe so. Amid the turmoil present in this letter, there is hope!

Nearly two years after Paul had visited Corinth and launched the church there (ca. AD 50–51), the believers knew they were neck-deep in conflict and, as a result, the following ensued:

1. The believers wrote Paul a letter, asking him for advice on several ethical and theological matters. Sadly, this letter is lost;

2. Paul responded to their letter with one often dubbed "Proto-Corinthians" (1 Cor. 5:9). This letter, also lost, did not satisfy the recipients; thus,

3. Some from the congregation wrote again, seeking clarification and further detail. Chloe, who hosted worship gatherings, along with some from her house, carried the letter to Paul and offered additional explanation;

4. Paul responded from Ephesus with 1 Corinthians around AD 53–54 (16:8, 19–21) and;

5. Knowing that the fledgling Christian gathering was in a state of flux, Paul tells them that he has his heart set on returning. Paul, however, with tears, was resigned to writing another letter—2 Corinthians—because he had trouble reaching them (2 Cor. 1:15–16; 2:1; 9:5; 12:14; 13:1). His failure to visit had relationally damaging effects.

Some in Corinth concluded that Paul was wishy-washy and could not be trusted; he couldn't keep his word. This led them to question the validity of his apostleship. When he speaks of the "thorn in his flesh" (2 Cor. 12:7), he is referring to repeated and painful attacks on his apostolic standing. His hope that his letters would be an effective stand-in for his absence was only partially realized. In Paul's world, honor and shame carried great cultural currency. He did not shy away from exposing darkness. Shame was a powerful motivator, and he believed it could lead to repentance. When we read 1 Corinthians today, we would do well to remember that and, perhaps, even imitate Paul in this regard. And we can be certain of one thing: that's not the kind of advice you'll hear on television today.

ONE

Better Call Paul

1 Corinthians 1:1–3 CEB *From Paul, called by God's will to be an apostle of Jesus Christ, and from Sosthenes our brother.*
²To God's church that is in Corinth:
To those who have been made holy to God in Christ Jesus, who are called to be God's people.
Together with all those who call upon the name of our Lord Jesus Christ in every place—he's their Lord and ours!
³Grace to you and peace from God our Father and the Lord Jesus Christ.

Key Observation. The only appropriate and worthy response to God's grace is devoting one's life to him.

Understanding the Word. Today, letter writing is a lost art. Text messaging and e-mail have nearly pushed the handwritten letter to extinction. Yet, when someone writes a letter, it tells you that they took an extended amount of time to think about you. It's a bit more tangible.

Paul was a thinker and a letter writer. A native of Tarsus, he was educated under a well-known Jewish teacher named Gamaliel. In 1 Corinthians 1:1, Paul, along with another Jewish teacher, Sosthenes, who himself may have been a synagogue leader in Corinth, sends greetings. Sosthenes may have carried 1 Corinthians from Ephesus to Corinth.

Prior to his Damascus Road encounter, Paul was the ancient equivalent of a modern-day terrorist. He was zealous for his faith. He may have killed Christians whom he thought had defiled Judaism. He sought to purify the land and the religion of his forefathers by cleansing it of these impurities.

Things changed, however, on the Damascus Road. Soon thereafter, the apostle received his call from the Lord. That call was spoken to Paul through Ananias: "This man is my chosen instrument to proclaim my name to the Gentiles and their kings and to the people of Israel. I will show him how much he must suffer for my name" (Acts 9:15–16). For Paul, to be called was not simply a fancy way of cloaking his own desires in Christianese. To be called was to suffer as an apostle.

The essence of apostleship meant putting one's life on the line for Christ. Paul eschewed violence. He turned to peacemaking. This was God's sanctifying will. Paul tells those in Corinth that they, too, were *called* to sanctification, to *be holy people*. Holiness and sanctification belong together. Holiness has to do with one's proximity to God. Sanctification has to do with the posture of one's heart toward God, others, self, and creation.

Such a life is seasoned with grace and peace. These two words form an idiomatic greeting for Paul. The word *grace* was a Greek economic term dealing with giving and receiving. Grace *always* expected to be met with a return of grace—it was never one-sided. Any sign of cheap grace—taking advantage of someone's grace without a worthy response—was viewed as shameful. Peace, in Hebrew thought, dealt with being whole and in healthy relational standing. Paul has two hopes in this greeting to Greeks, Jews, and others in Corinth:

(1) to create unity, and (2) to remind them that Jesus, their gift from the Father, is not cheap but requires a worthy response. The only worthy response is to devote one's life to God.

1. What is the relationship between holiness and sanctification?
2. What is cheap grace and why is it problematic?

TWO
Thank God

1 Corinthians 1:4–9 CEB *I thank my God always for you, because of God's grace that was given to you in Christ Jesus. ⁵That is, you were made rich through him in everything: in all your communication and every kind of knowledge, ⁶in the same way that the testimony about Christ was confirmed with you. ⁷The result is that you aren't missing any spiritual gift while you wait for our Lord Jesus Christ to be revealed. ⁸He will also confirm your testimony about Christ until the end so that you will be blameless on the day of our Lord Jesus Christ. ⁹God is faithful, and you were called by him to partnership with his Son, Jesus Christ our Lord.*

Key Observation. Actions speak loudest alongside one's words.

Understanding the Word. Most folks appreciate the value of a genuine thank you. Unfortunately, such remarks come much too rarely. My children are, for the most part, respectful and well-mannered. I, as a parent, however, find it difficult to imagine them bursting forth with unprompted remarks of gratitude all the time. Nevertheless, a well-timed word of appreciation from them can go a long way.

In thinking about Paul's comment here regarding giving thanks, well, it is a bit jarring. Paul views himself as a spiritual parent to the believers in Corinth (e.g., 1 Cor. 4:14). As such, he wields the pen of discipline and puts his children in their place (3:1; 14:20, etc.). He masterfully balances giving thanks with giving correctives. It is exhausting to practice "always" being thankful for those in our lives, especially for those who consistently choose to live outside the call and will of God. That can be incredibly difficult and painful to witness.

Paul suggests that those in Corinth had received everything from God they needed. God, for instance, had enriched them with gifts of speech and knowledge. These two words surface repeatedly throughout the epistle. In fact, much of the schism occurring within the assembly orbited around them.

Paul confronts these matters early, letting the congregants know they will not weasel their way out of accountability. In his mind, because God gave them these gifts and they happily received them, a holy and worthy response is expected. God's gifts were not (and still are not!) meant to divide. Instead, they are given to help believers *stand firm*, *be blameless*, and live out their calling *in fellowship* with Jesus and one another.

Notice, too, that Paul offers several references to the end here. His comments are not meant to cause believers to look to the future but to examine the here-and-now. God's gracious gifts will sustain believers and firm them up in the present. As long as a believer remains open to the sanctifying work of God, they can rest assured that he will continue working in and among them. Moreover, it is one's firm stance in the gospel that bears evidence of Jesus's work. Paul says that one's steadfastness is a confirmation that God *was* at work in Jesus and *is* at work in his people (1:6).

Thus, it's not that "actions speak louder than words," but "actions speak loudest *alongside* one's words." It is a fallacy to pit actions against words; both matter and are foundational to the gospel. Actions void of words collapse into mere social work. Social work is a good thing but is not the whole gospel. Likewise, words without actions tend to result in mere lip service. Thus, actions and words must be held together. Neither, however, can be done without sincere conviction and a strong backbone—two things that, thankfully, God himself is willing to give us.

1. How does Paul strike a balance in being thankful for the Christians in Corinth on the one hand and doling out discipline to them on the other?
2. For Christians, the old saying "Actions speak louder than words" is always true. How does Paul's thinking qualify such a statement?

Week One

THREE
United Way

1 Corinthians 1:10 CEB *Now I encourage you, brothers and sisters, in the name of our Lord Jesus Christ: Agree with each other and don't be divided into rival groups. Instead, be restored with the same mind and the same purpose.*

Key Observation. Unity is only achievable by working together in Jesus's name.

Understanding the Word. Christianity has never really experienced a golden age, a time of pure, unadulterated, and perfect existence. Instead, the church has always been broken and messy. Church history reveals this a hundredfold. Why? Because the church has always been full of broken people with messy lives.

Of course, the body of Christ has had its moments of beauty and fleeting perfection. The church has done much good for the world. There have been times when God's people have turned to Scripture, repented, extended forgiveness, and gotten on with the business of taking the whole gospel to the whole world. Such instances are where orthopraxy (right living) meets orthodoxy (right believing). This meeting has real-world consequences.

For instance, Paul's remarks in 1 Corinthians 1:10 are akin to a thesis statement for the entire epistle. His plea is for the church at Corinth to overcome discord with concord. Such a feat is accomplished not by threatening, bartering behind closed doors, or pushing a pet agenda. Unity is only achievable by working together in Jesus's name.

Those who consider themselves members of God's family have essentially taken on Jesus's name (see Rev. 3:12). Paul applies sibling language to every believer in Roman Corinth. While this is often described as "fictive kinship" terminology—a social-scientific term used to denote fake family ties rather than those by bloodline or marriage—such a descriptor is seriously misguided. Christ's blood, which covers confessed sinners and unites the body of Christ, is thicker than blood inherent to one's genetic bloodline. The kinship connections in Christianity are anything but fictive. As an insider, Paul strategically employs such language to *speak* as frankly as he does.

As noted previously, speech and knowledge are focal elements throughout the letter and rest at the heart of the congregation's divisions. That is reiterated here. Instead of being passive-aggressive, Paul tackles the issue head on. He tells those in Corinth who bore the name of Jesus Christ that divisions must go. In place of those divisions must be agreement regarding everything said and thought *in the name of Jesus Christ* by those *bearing the name of Jesus Christ*.

The apostle did not have in mind trivial agreements. He desired perfect agreement about the preached gospel; otherwise, division would not only remain, it would reign. Paul is issuing a clarion call to return to the gospel. Two thousand years later, it's still apropos. Yet, many who desire to be united are among the most divided; they are not the united "Way" (Acts 22:4). My diagnosis: the gospel has been mutilated by some, resulting in a bankrupt form of orthopraxy and orthodoxy. My hope: we will find the courage to embrace repentance and cling to the gospel handed on to us by Paul, our big brother (1 Cor. 15:1–3ff).

1. How does 1 Corinthians 1:10 function like a thesis statement for the whole letter?
2. What, as a Christian, are some of the implications of taking on Jesus's name as one's own?

FOUR
Troublin' the Waters

1 Corinthians 1:11–17 CEB *My brothers and sisters, Chloe's people gave me some information about you, that you're fighting with each other. ¹²What I mean is this: that each one of you says, "I belong to Paul," "I belong to Apollos," "I belong to Cephas," "I belong to Christ." ¹³Has Christ been divided? Was Paul crucified for you, or were you baptized in Paul's name? ¹⁴Thank God that I didn't baptize any of you, except Crispus and Gaius, ¹⁵so that nobody can say that you were baptized in my name! ¹⁶Oh, I baptized the house of Stephanas too. Otherwise, I don't know if I baptized anyone else. ¹⁷Christ didn't send me to baptize but to preach the good news. And Christ didn't send me to preach the good news with clever words so that Christ's cross won't be emptied of its meaning.*

Key Observation. Faulty theology leads to division.

Understanding the Word. I can usually tell if my children are lying. Yet, it is often difficult to tell who is speaking the truth when one says something happened one way and the other has an alternative story. Trying to officiate an ongoing contest of one-upmanship is taxing. Sometimes I stop the game and call a time out for the kids involved.

Paul, of course, couldn't confine his bickering letter recipients to a Corinthian corner. But, eleven verses in, he pauses the game. The "brothers and sisters" who have been given every unifying gift by God, had started causing divisions. They had completely misidentified the source of their spiritual gifts. This deserves explanation.

In 1:12 Paul quotes several statements uttered by factions within Corinth. Some claimed to follow Paul, some Apollos, and some Cephas (i.e., Peter). In 1:13–17, Paul mentions that while he baptized some, he did not baptize everyone. Apollos and Cephas also baptized some. Problems arose when congregants began arguing that their baptisms took on meaning based on who did the baptizing—Paul, Apollos, Peter, or, in a show of true arrogance, a spiritual baptism by Jesus.

For them, being baptized by a certain leader resulted in specific types of spiritual gifts. A baptism by Paul might result in the gift of prophecy. Baptism by Peter might result in the gift of evangelizing. Whatever gift the baptizing apostle had, the one being baptized might receive. Divisive speech was fueling the creation of Corinthian cliques, but Paul hoped that unity would win the day.

He started the church in Corinth. He knew and evangelized these people. He taught and baptized some of them. While it may appear that Paul is devaluing baptism here, he is not. Paul had a high view of baptism. He says he's glad he didn't baptize more people because he knows, in retrospect, that it would have troubled the waters even more. It would have meant more wrong-headed views about baptism, baptizers, and gifts.

For Gentile converts in the early church, baptism came after many catechetical classes. Catechesis consisted of formally teaching new believers the basics of the faith. It ended with baptismal initiation into the body of Christ. Jews, however, who were already immersed in the story of Israel, often underwent baptism much sooner. Paul stayed in Corinth for two to three years during his initial visit (Acts 18:11–18)—ample time for catechizing and baptizing.

Paul's main role wasn't to stick around and catechize or baptize. He was, mainly, a church planter. Others (e.g., Apollos, Peter, etc.) did the catechizing and baptizing. What Paul is downplaying is *a faulty view* of baptism. His analysis of the cascading turmoil in Corinth reveals just how easily and quickly wrong beliefs can lead to wrong actions and devastate the church. When this happens, the church voids the power of the cross in their lives and testimonies. Orthodoxy and orthopraxy matter. Let us remember, then: it doesn't just pay to cling to the cross, it also costs!

1. Why is it important to understand that Paul is not downplaying baptism in 1 Corinthians?
2. How are cliques being formed within the Corinthian assembly?

FIVE

Four Big Buts

1 Corinthians 1:18–25 *For the message of the cross is foolishness to those who are perishing, but to us who are being saved it is the power of God.* [19]*For it is written:*

"I will destroy the wisdom of the wise;
the intelligence of the intelligent I will frustrate."

[20]*Where is the wise person? Where is the teacher of the law? Where is the philosopher of this age? Has not God made foolish the wisdom of the world?* [21]*For since in the wisdom of God the world through its wisdom did not know him, God was pleased through the foolishness of what was preached to save those who believe.* [22]*Jews demand signs and Greeks look for wisdom,* [23]*but we preach Christ crucified: a stumbling block to Jews and foolishness to Gentiles,* [24]*but to those whom God has called, both Jews and Greeks, Christ the power of God and the wisdom of God.* [25]*For the foolishness of God is wiser than human wisdom, and the weakness of God is stronger than human strength.*

Key Observation. There should be a noticeable difference in the lives of those perishing and those being saved.

Understanding the Word. One day several years ago, I had a friend invite me to lunch. When I arrived, we shook hands, exchanged greetings, and caught up. It was going great until he dropped a bomb: "Michael, it's good to see you, *but* I'm going to say something that could potentially damage our friendship." I'll refrain from filling in the details. The point is: I experienced that awkward moment when someone's kind words were immediately followed with and negated by a big *but*.

In this passage, while only three "buts" appear in the NIV translation, in Greek there are four (1 Cor. 1:18, 23 (2x), 24). These buts accentuate Paul's point by way of contrast: foolish/wise, Jew/Gentile, God/humans, weakness/strength, and perishing/being saved. In 1:18 Paul says, "For the message of the cross is foolishness to those who are perishing *but* to us who are being saved it is the power of God." The "for" reveals a connection to the preceding statement about not feuding over who baptized whom, and not preaching in a manner that empties the cross of its power. Paul's contrast is between outsiders and insiders; he is among the latter. He says there should be a noticeable difference between those perishing and those being saved. (Note, by the way, that "being saved" is not spoken of in the past tense here but the present—salvation is to be worked out in the present.)

The apostle's next two buts appear in 1:23. A more accurate translation is: "Jews demand signs and Greeks look for wisdom, *but* we preach Christ crucified: on the one hand, it is a stumbling block to the Jews *but*, on the other hand, foolishness to the Gentiles." In 1:3, Paul strategically uses a Jewish-Gentile greeting meant to signal unity. Here he addresses both again. What they think they "know" about the gospel was deficient and it was affecting how they lived. This, then, is where "knowledge" along with "speech" began to factor into the problems present in Corinth. The last *but* seems to be the continuation of the interrupted thought in 1:23: "*but* we preach Christ crucified, Christ the power of God and wisdom of God."

Jews and Gentiles who have not been persuaded by Paul's preaching regard it as foolishness. In Paul's view, however, God's power and wisdom were displayed on the cross, which was not necessarily the way one might have expected the Almighty to act. But then again, humans, even on their best days, cannot hold a candle to the wisdom and strength of God. When they do, they only end up looking foolish. There are no ifs, ands, or *buts* about that!

1. What are the implications of Paul's view of salvation, namely, that believers are in the process of "being saved"?
2. How is knowledge, which Paul alludes to early in the letter, contributing to schism within the Corinthian congregation?

WEEK ONE

GATHERING DISCUSSION OUTLINE

A. **Open session in prayer.** Ask that God would astonish us anew with fresh insight from God's Word and transform us into the disciples that Jesus desires us to become.

B. **View video for this week's readings.**

C. **Ask:** What were key insights or takeaways that you gained from your reading during the week and from watching the video commentary? In particular, how did these help you to grow in your faith and understanding of Scripture this week? What parts of the Bible lesson or study raised questions for you?

D. **Discuss questions selected from the daily readings.**

   1. **KEY OBSERVATION:** The only appropriate and worthy response to God's grace is devoting one's life to him.

      DISCUSSION QUESTION: What is cheap grace and why is it problematic?

   2. **KEY OBSERVATION:** Actions speak loudest alongside one's words.

      DISCUSSION QUESTION: For Christians, the old saying "Actions speak louder than words" is always true. How does Paul's thinking qualify such a statement?

   3. **KEY OBSERVATION:** Unity is only achievable by working together in Jesus's name.

DISCUSSION QUESTION: What, as a Christian, are some of the implications of taking on Jesus's name as one's own?

4. **KEY OBSERVATION:** Faulty theology leads to division.

    DISCUSSION QUESTION: Why is it important to understand that Paul is not downplaying baptism in 1 Corinthians?

5. **KEY OBSERVATION:** There should be a noticeable difference in the lives of those perishing and those being saved.

    DISCUSSION QUESTION: What are the implications of Paul's view of salvation, namely, that believers are in the process of "being saved"?

E. **As the study concludes, consider specific ways that this week's Bible lesson invites you to grow and calls you to change.** How do this week's scriptures call us to think differently? How do they challenge us to change in order to align ourselves with God's work in the world? What specific actions should we take to apply the insights of the lesson into our daily lives? What kind of person does our Bible lesson call us to become?

F. **Close session with prayer.** Emphasize God's ongoing work of transformation in our lives in preparation for loving mission and service in the world. Pray for absent class members as well as for persons whom we need to invite to join our study.

WEEK TWO

1 Corinthians 1:26–3:32
No Cracks in the Foundation

INTRODUCTION

Numerous themes found in 1 Corinthians 1:1–25 also appear in this week's verses (1:26–3:32). We see Paul, once again, zeroing in on division's threats to unity. He reiterates the fact that spiritual gifts, social status, and a fundamental misunderstanding of the gospel are cutting to the core of the congregation in Corinth. While the foundation that he laid cannot be changed (otherwise it will not be the same foundation!), it does appear that cracks are beginning to form.

It is a powerful analogy. Today, some are attempting to either take a jackhammer to or pave over the longstanding gospel foundation that Paul laid. That, however, is all in vain. Any new foundation attempting to replace the apostolic one, handed down through historic Christianity, is unworthy of building upon. Such a foundation is weak, deficient, and nothing more than a façade that will come crashing down. In our society, cultural fads are plentiful. Acts of modifying the gospel to avoid social ostracism or persecution abound. A clarion call needs to be reissued to the church. When read with fully open eyes and ears, Paul's epistle does just that.

ONE

Ones upon a Time

1 Corinthians 1:26–31 *Brothers and sisters, think of what you were when you were called. Not many of you were wise by human standards; not many were influential; not many were of noble birth. ²⁷But God chose the foolish [ones] of* *the world to shame the wise; God chose the weak [ones] of the world to shame the strong. ²⁸God chose the lowly [ones] of this world and the despised [ones]—and the [ones] that are not—to nullify the [ones] that are, ²⁹so that no one may boast before him. ³⁰It is because of him that you are in Christ Jesus, who has become for us wisdom from God—that is, our righteousness, holiness and redemption. ³¹Therefore, as it is written: "Let the one who boasts boast in the Lord."*

Key Observation. God's wisdom, manifest in Jesus's life, is this: sacrifice for one another.

Understanding the Word. First Corinthians 1:26–31 can be translated various ways. Unlike the NIV, which uses the word "things" (e.g., foolish/weak/lowly/despised things, things that are not, things that are), I think it is more appropriate to use "ones," which I have done. This dramatically changes *things*. It provides insights about the identities of congregants. Understanding the social demographic helps make sense of why Paul says what he does the way he does. We already know about problems within the Corinthian assembly related to the abuse of gifts of speech and knowledge. Some thought they had received these gifts by being baptized by certain church leaders (e.g., Paul, Peter, or Apollos). As a result, they began attaching levels of social status to their gifts. This led to rank (in both senses of the word!) arguments.

In 1:26 Paul describes those in Corinth as: (1) siblings; (2) "called" by God; (3) some not too wise by human standards; (4) some not too socially influential; and (5) some not born with a high status. Points 1 and 2 contrast with 3–5. In Corinth, status and honor could be acquired or ascribed. One could be born with high status and honor or try to earn it. Paul says that not many there were born with ascribed honor. Some, however, had acquired it. Paul calls those who have moved up the social cline to remember what they once were. They should recall that they were once like those whom they were lording their status over. Siblings in the Lord do not act that way.

Even more, Paul suggests that the non-elite share the same status as the elite. Why? Because they were siblings called by the same God. Those perceived as higher are no better than the lower. The foolish share their status and call with the wise. These same fools, also referred to as the weak, the lowly, the despised, and the nothings, have been used and called by God. The gospel is the great social equalizer; all are social equals, and no one is left to boast before

God (1:29). Boasting about Christ is the only acceptable form of boasting in the Lord (1:31). Paul says that Jesus became wisdom from God to us (1:30). God's wisdom, manifest in Jesus's life, is this: sacrifice for one another. Wisdom from God is not taking his gifts, using them for selfish advancement, and causing division. Also, in confounding our self-absorbed ways, he became righteousness (right standing with God), holiness, and redemption.

The term *redemption* comes from the ancient marketplace. It has to do with making a payment. Like "ransom," it is tricky in a theological sense. If Jesus was our redemption/ransom, to whom was the payment made? God the Father? Satan? Someone else? Here's one explanation: by way of sin, humanity handed itself over to Satan. Satan thought humans were his to keep. He, having hold of God's people, sought to negotiate with God. The Father must give up Jesus in exchange for them. In this, and in Jesus's crucifixion, Satan thought he had won a bargain (see Matt. 4:1–11; Mark 1:12–13). When Jesus was raised, however, Satan's supposed win was shown to be null and void. In the resurrection, Jesus conquered Satan, sin, and death, and reclaimed his people, including those of this passage.

1. How does God's wisdom undermine and oppose the wisdom of this world?
2. In what ways might the social differences in the Corinthian assembly be contributing to the problems there?

TWO

Rulers Not Measuring Up

1 Corinthians 2:1–8 ESV *And I, when I came to you, brothers, did not come proclaiming to you the testimony of God with lofty speech or wisdom. ²For I decided to know nothing among you except Jesus Christ and him crucified. ³And I was with you in weakness and in fear and much trembling, ⁴and my speech and my message were not in plausible words of wisdom, but in demonstration of the Spirit and of power, ⁵so that your faith might not rest in the wisdom of men but in the power of God.*

⁶Yet among the mature we do impart wisdom, although it is not a wisdom of this age or of the rulers of this age, who are doomed to pass away. ⁷But we impart a secret and hidden wisdom of God, which God decreed before the ages for our glory. ⁸None of the rulers of this age understood this, for if they had, they would not have crucified the Lord of glory.

Key Observation. Followers of Jesus must live cruciform lives.

Understanding the Word. Peoples' words say a lot about what is going on in their lives. In 1 Corinthians, Paul often begins a thought by addressing his audience as siblings. He then goes on to offer stark contrasts. He does that in this passage, just as he did in several sections of the preceding chapter. The apostle has already noted deep-seated divisions within the assembly. The believers, like Paul's words, are clashing.

One important contrast has to do with the fact that Paul did not initially come to Corinth in the likeness of a used car salesman—with flashy rhetoric and stellar showmanship. Instead, he came in weakness, with fear and trembling, having the appearance of one who was unwise and unpersuasive. Paul is not being self-deprecating to gain pity but highlighting the fact that he lives as one being crucified with Christ daily.

In Paul's society, honor was a hot commodity, but not everyone could attain it. Shame, the inverse, was to be avoided at all costs. Part of living a cruciform life, one conformed to the shape of the cross, is embodying the willingness to sacrifice one's life for the gospel. Paul admits that this is a scary proposition. It can strike fear and trembling into a person. Even Jesus wasn't beyond this fear (Mark 14:36; Luke 22:42).

Paul's "testimony about God" was not one delivered with an iron fist. Neither does he lace his messages with empty rhetorical flourish. Had he desired, he could have approached the Corinthians with high-style rhetoric. When he first met them, however, his preaching was not of that sort. Instead, he endured suffering because of it. As such, the content of his preaching focused on Christ's suffering and how we should be ready to endure when it befalls us. Following a suffering, crucified God seems unwise. Further, to those who view themselves as elites, a life riddled with suffering is unpersuasive. Wouldn't a powerful God spare himself and his followers pain and suffering? How could a true God be conquered by the rulers of this world? What is enticing about this type of thinking? Well, for the apostle, those who believe themselves to be powerful in the here-and-now are being made powerless by a gospel that calls its adherents to self-sacrifice, submission, and serving one another.

1. What does it mean to live a cruciform life?
2. How does the apostle's critique of the "rulers of this age" fit into the argument presented here?

THREE
Reality Check

1 Corinthians 2:9–16 ESV *But, as it is written,*
"What no eye has seen, nor ear heard,
 nor the heart of man imagined,
what God has prepared for those who love him"—
[10]these things God has revealed to us through the Spirit. For the Spirit searches everything, even the depths of God. [11]For who knows a person's thoughts except the spirit of that person, which is in him? So also no one comprehends the thoughts of God except the Spirit of God. [12]Now we have received not the spirit of the world, but the Spirit who is from God, that we might understand the things freely given us by God. [13]And we impart this in words not taught by human wisdom but taught by the Spirit, interpreting spiritual truths to those who are spiritual.

[14]The natural person does not accept the things of the Spirit of God, for they are folly to him, and he is not able to understand them because they are spiritually discerned. [15]The spiritual person judges all things, but is himself to be judged by no one. [16]"For who has understood the mind of the Lord so as to instruct him?" But we have the mind of Christ.

Key Observation. The Holy Spirit reveals the mind of Christ to believers and, in so doing, shapes their thoughts and words.

Understanding the Word. In recent years, the fad of finding Jesus-shaped silhouettes in grilled cheese sandwiches has been on the rise. These grilled cheeses (not grilled Jesuses!) often take the Internet by storm; they go viral and spark amazement. Folks, of course, have claimed to find such images elsewhere: cloud formations, tree rings, rocks, grease build-ups in skillets, Cheetos, and even fur patterns on dogs' rear ends. As interesting (or off-putting!) as looking for Jesus in such places might be, one fact remains: the first and best place to find Jesus is in Scripture.

The second? In the exemplary lives of his followers. Their lives should be patterned after his. In this section of 1 Corinthians, Paul makes a few fascinating claims. One is that Christ's followers have the mind of Christ. Another, related to the first, is that the Spirit indwells God's people. Moreover, the Spirit reveals the mind of Christ to them and teaches them to speak Spirit-taught words. Paul contends that Christian life orbits around these two ideas.

Let's attempt to follow a bit of Paul's logic. He says: (1) the Spirit of God knows the thoughts of God (i.e., the mind of Christ); (2) the Spirit of God dwells in us; (3) thus, the Spirit gives us access to the thoughts of God; and (4) the Spirit of God enables and equips us to speak Spirit-taught words. This spiritual reality is also the real-life reality of believers. To earnestly believe that we have access to the thoughts of God/the mind of Christ should be a major wake-up call. It should be a reality check. This is even more jolting when we recall that speech and knowledge are two issues at the heart of the divisions among the Corinthian believers.

Paul brackets this entire discussion between two Old Testament quotations. The first is from Isaiah 64:4: "Since ancient times no one has heard, no ear has perceived, no eye has seen any God besides you, who acts on behalf of those who wait for him." He continues, suggesting that those who remember God's ways please God; however, those who sin against him, move him to anger. Paul says that the rulers in the verses preceding this section have worked against God and, in so doing, have created division. Those whom God has blessed, however, should be working together. When they do, the Spirit will bring about unity. If they resist this, they are essentially nothing more than power-mongers becoming powerless.

The second quotation is from Isaiah 40:13–14. It fits well within this passage: "Who can fathom the Spirit of the Lord or instruct the Lord as his counselor? Whom did the Lord consult to enlighten him, and who taught him the right way? Who was it that taught him knowledge, or showed him the path of understanding?" The context is similar. Yet, the questions asked here, which are all rhetorical in nature, expect "Nobody!" as their answer.

By default, all true wisdom, knowledge, and understanding reside in the Lord. All wisdom, knowledge, and understanding stem from God. In forgetting this, humans tend to boast in themselves. This, in turn, creates an atmosphere ripe for division. This is part of what has happened in Corinth, and this is part of what is continuing to happen in the church thousands of years later. Whenever she strays from the thoughts of God/the mind of Christ, the church stands the risk of no longer being the church. Instead, she will collapse into a social club, political movement, or false religion. Indeed, she may even lapse into superstition and begin looking to grilled cheese sandwiches for a fresh word from God.

1. According to Paul, what are a couple core ideas that the Christian life orbits around?
2. What does it mean to have the thoughts of God/mind of Christ?

FOUR
Growing Pains

1 Corinthians 3:1–8 NABRE *Brothers, I could not talk to you as spiritual people, but as fleshly people, as infants in Christ. ²I fed you milk, not solid food, because you were unable to take it. Indeed, you are still not able, even now, ³for you are still of the flesh. While there is jealousy and rivalry among you, are you not of the flesh, and behaving in an ordinary human way? ⁴Whenever someone says, "I belong to Paul," and another, "I belong to Apollos," are you not merely human?*

⁵What is Apollos, after all, and what is Paul? Ministers through whom you became believers, just as the Lord assigned each one. ⁶I planted, Apollos watered, but God caused the growth. ⁷Therefore, neither the one who plants nor the one who waters is anything, but only God, who causes the growth. ⁸The one who plants and the one who waters are equal, and each will receive wages in proportion to his labor.

Key Observation. People have a choice to either walk in the godly or ungodly realm.

Understanding the Word. Siblings bicker, argue, tease, and push one another's buttons. When such in-house fighting occurs among children, oftentimes, they're over it a few minutes later and are back to playing together. It is astounding how quickly children forgive, forget, and move on together. Even with limited social skills, kids can navigate this part of life with ease. There is a deep beauty in this.

When those same siblings argue as adults, however, it often takes a long time to get over it. Forgiveness may not even be an option on the table. Adults, who typically have social skills, should be able to work through such things. Nevertheless, many siblings part ways as they age because they cannot get along. They move on without one other rather than together.

Paul is, unfortunately, talking more about the second type of scenario. The Corinthian Christians are splitting. They lack the skills to successfully navigate these choppy relational seas. They exhibit spiritual immaturity. Paul even calls them infants. Their infancy is a sign of adhering to worldly ways. Using the image of a mother or wet nurse, Paul also says that he has fed them milk. Might that have been embarrassing for them?

Paul has previously referred to them as "those sanctified in Christ Jesus and called to be his holy people" (1 Cor. 1:2). Here, however, he cannot address them as people who live by the Spirit. The comments in 1:2 are in the past tense while those in 3:1–2 are in the present. In other words, those in the congregation had, at the time of writing, stepped out of who they were in Christ to be something else.

This brings up questions of predestination. Many have argued that predestination refers to persons who were destined by God, before creation, to be included among those chosen by him for salvific purposes (or not). Such a view is wrong. When Paul talks about predestination, he is talking less about people and more about realms. In Paul's thinking, there is a dualism of realms—a spiritual/godly realm and a worldly/ungodly realm. Each realm had its own path and traits. Humans choose which realm they walk and live in.

Individuals can move in and out of realms at their choosing. As they do, they take on the traits of that realm. Further, each realm has a massive set of stock characteristics. The spiritual/godly realm, for instance, has the traits of wisdom, knowledge, sacrifice, and more. The worldly/ungodly realm has lying, cheating, selfishness, and more. In fact, an entire Christian literary tradition known as "The Two Ways Tradition" developed from this. It is found in the New Testament and an early second-century document titled *The Didache*.

Alongside his milk-giving metaphor, Paul also uses a gardening metaphor. He says that he planted the congregation, Apollos watered, and God brought the growth. But there had been much less growth than Paul had hoped for. This, however, was not God's fault. The blame fell on the Corinthians. They had chosen to walk in the worldly realm, closing themselves off to God. Paul's call is for them to get back on track—to step back into the spiritual realm.

The point of the various metaphors is this: when appropriate, Paul will treat those in Corinth like siblings. At other times, he may need to treat them like little children. Still, at other times, he may need to remind them that he planted them and, as such, remains invested in seeing them grow up. He may need to discipline them. Growing pains are difficult. They are easier to navigate, however, when everyone's on the same path, walking together in the same spiritual/godly realm.

1. If the believers in Corinth are already confused about Paul, what benefit might there have been in the apostle using several images (e.g., sibling, parent/wet nurse, planter) to speak about himself? Could this have contributed to the confusion?

2. What are some traits inherent to the godly and ungodly realms?

FIVE

Made in Corinth

1 Corinthians 3:9–23 NABRE *For we are God's co-workers; you are God's field, God's building.*

[10]According to the grace of God given to me, like a wise master builder I laid a foundation, and another is building upon it. But each one must be careful how he builds upon it, [11]for no one can lay a foundation other than the one that is there, namely, Jesus Christ. [12]If anyone builds on this foundation with gold, silver, precious stones, wood, hay, or straw, [13]the work of each will come to light, for the Day will disclose it. It will be revealed with fire, and the fire [itself] will test the quality of each one's work. [14]If the work stands that someone built upon the

foundation, that person will receive a wage. ¹⁵*But if someone's work is burned up, that one will suffer loss; the person will be saved, but only as through fire.* ¹⁶*Do you not know that you are the temple of God, and that the Spirit of God dwells in you?* ¹⁷*If anyone destroys God's temple, God will destroy that person; for the temple of God, which you are, is holy.*

¹⁸*Let no one deceive himself. If anyone among you considers himself wise in this age, let him become a fool so as to become wise.* ¹⁹*For the wisdom of this world is foolishness in the eyes of God, for it is written:*

"He catches the wise in their own ruses,"

²⁰*and again:*

"The Lord knows the thoughts of the wise, that they are vain."

²¹*So let no one boast about human beings, for everything belongs to you,* ²²*Paul or Apollos or Cephas, or the world or life or death, or the present or the future: all belong to you,* ²³*and you to Christ, and Christ to God.*

Key Observation. The gospel must always remain the foundation of the church.

Understanding the Word. Have you ever met someone whose story always tops yours? A person you cannot engage in genuine conversation because they are always attempting to one-up you? A person who was hurt worse, ate the most, slept the least, ran the fastest, climbed the highest, or made more money? I'm sure you've met someone like that.

The highlighted passage, which brings us to the end of chapter 3, is the point where Paul had simply had enough of the one-up games in Corinth. He says to believers in 3:21, "So, then, no more boasting about human leaders!" In other words, stop saying things along the lines of, "I was baptized by Paul, inherited Paul's spiritual gift(s), and am better than you because of it." Paul states that everyone in the assembly should view themselves as coworkers. While he employs field imagery 3:6–8, he proceeds to use a house/building image here.

Paul says that he was a great builder. This is evidenced by the faith foundation that he laid in Corinth. That foundation is firm. It never changes. If anything replaces it, it is no longer the true foundation. In the event of a fire, everything built on top of the foundation will burn. When it does, however, the firm foundation will remain. It does not burn. The firm foundation holds the building up.

Although Paul lays the foundation (i.e., the gospel) in Corinth, at the time of writing, he is gone. In his absence, others are attempting to build upon the foundation. They are not doing a great job. In fact, cracks are starting to form. If it gets to the point where the foundation is weakened to uselessness, then it is not the builder's fault. The blame goes to those who caused the rifts. In short, if the Christians in Corinth attempted to blame Paul for the sorry state that they're in, he only needed to point to the foundation. He can then say, "Look! The foundation's still there. Continue building on that and you will be safe. Build elsewhere, however, and you will regret it."

Paul, of course, is not speaking of a literal building that he has built. He is talking about the congregation in Corinth—God's people, God's temple. This would have been an astonishing remark to Jewish persons in the congregation. It came, after all, nearly two decades before the sacking of the Jerusalem temple in AD 70. Paul is already insinuating, following Jesus's teachings, that God's Spirit had evacuated the Jerusalem temple and relocated. He had taken up residence in believers.

The Spirit has indwelt all believers, without distinction. Thus, no one has the right or ability to argue about whose spiritual gift or status received at baptism is greatest. No more arguing about that! Paul says that he, Apollos, and Cephas (i.e., Peter) are all servants of those in Corinth. Likewise, the Corinthians were servants of Christ. Christ was a servant of God the Father (see Acts 3:26; Phil. 2:7). This model of servanthood begins, oddly enough, not at the top, but the bottom. Servanthood is a trait indicative of a mature believer walking in the spiritual/godly realm.

1. What would you say, according to the first three chapters of 1 Corinthians, is the greatest issue threatening the congregation thus far?

2. Based on the first three chapters of 1 Corinthians, what would you say Paul's foundation consists of?

WEEK TWO

GATHERING DISCUSSION OUTLINE

A. **Open session in prayer.** Ask that God would astonish us anew with fresh insight from God's Word and transform us into the disciples that Jesus desires us to become.

B. **View video for this week's readings.**

C. **Ask:** What were key insights or takeaways that you gained from your reading during the week and from watching the video commentary? In particular, how did these help you to grow in your faith and understanding of Scripture this week? What parts of the Bible lesson or study raised questions for you?

D. **Discuss questions selected from the daily readings.**

   1. **KEY OBSERVATION:** God's wisdom, manifest in Jesus's life, is this: sacrifice for one another.

      DISCUSSION QUESTION: How does God's wisdom undermine and oppose the wisdom of this world?

   2. **KEY OBSERVATION:** Followers of Jesus must live cruciform lives.

      DISCUSSION QUESTION: What does it mean to live a cruciform life?

   3. **KEY OBSERVATION:** The Holy Spirit reveals the mind of Christ to believers and, in so doing, shapes their thoughts and words.

      DISCUSSION QUESTION: What does it mean to have the thoughts of God/mind of Christ?

4. **KEY OBSERVATION:** People have a choice to either walk in the godly or ungodly realm.

   DISCUSSION QUESTION: What are some traits inherent to the godly and ungodly realms?

5. **KEY OBSERVATION:** The gospel must always remain the foundation of the church.

   DISCUSSION QUESTION: Based on the first three chapters of 1 Corinthians, what would you say Paul's foundation consists of?

E. **As the study concludes, consider specific ways that this week's Bible lesson invites you to grow and calls you to change.** How do this week's scriptures call us to think differently? How do they challenge us to change in order to align ourselves with God's work in the world? What specific actions should we take to apply the insights of the lesson into our daily lives? What kind of person does our Bible lesson call us to become?

F. **Close session with prayer.** Emphasize God's ongoing work of transformation in our lives in preparation for loving mission and service in the world. Pray for absent class members as well as for persons whom we need to invite to join our study.

WEEK THREE

1 Corinthians 4:1–21

Paul's Apology

INTRODUCTION

In the first four chapters, Paul focuses on two main issues: (1) eradicating divisions and achieving unity; and (2) offering an apology/defense of himself as an apostle. In 4:1–21 his aim is to clear up gross misunderstandings about his identity. Some had errantly identified him as their leader, their baptizer with certain spiritual gifts and social status. Paul rejects that.

Paul also finds their claims about him not being a man of his word problematic. He tells them he would come again, but they did not believe him. As we shall see, some started rumors about this. Paul contends that arrogance was at the root of such fallacious thinking. His self-defense reached its climax here in the fourth chapter. Still, a broader picture may prove beneficial. Here is an outline of the epistle arranged in thematic blocks:

- 1:1–4:21: Plea for unity and apology/defense;
- 5:1–7:1: Answers to questions about sexuality, marriage, divorce, celibacy, etc.;
- 8:1–11:1: Answers to questions about eating in temples;
- 11:2–34: Answers to questions about proper worship;
- 12:1–14:40: Answers to questions about spiritual gifts;
- 15:1–58: Answers to questions about resurrection; and,
- 16:1–24: Remarks about the collection and his itinerary.

The bulk of Paul's epistle is concerned with answering questions raised by the Corinthians. Sometimes, when he seems to anticipate future critiques, Paul goes on the offensive and, instead of waiting for another letter, provides answers in the present. These are great teaching moments for Paul. The question is: Would the believers in Corinth pay attention and take note?

ONE

Can't Judge This

1 Corinthians 4:1–5 NET *One should think about us this way—as servants of Christ and stewards of the mysteries of God. ²Now what is sought in stewards is that one be found faithful. ³So for me, it is a minor matter that I am judged by you or by any human court. In fact, I do not even judge myself. ⁴For I am not aware of anything against myself, but I am not acquitted because of this. The one who judges me is the Lord. ⁵So then, do not judge anything before the time. Wait until the Lord comes. He will bring to light the hidden things of darkness and reveal the motives of hearts. Then each will receive recognition from God.*

Key Observation. Christians are called to help others see the error of their ways.

Understanding the Word. In America today, judging another's actions isn't tolerated. Folks chide Christians who make judgments about sins, sinful living, and sinful actions. Ironically, those same people often judge Christians as old-fashioned and out-of-touch with the twenty-first century. Some, based on religious convictions, disagree with same-sex marriage, abortion, war, the death penalty, and other such issues and, in very judgmental ways, are labeled bigots.

If someone wished to take Paul's words out of context, they could appeal to 1 Corinthians 4:5. They could argue that judging is wrong. The apostle says, "Therefore judge nothing before the appointed time; wait until the Lord comes." Does this mean that judging is completely off-limits until the Lord's return? No. Such a view contradicts Paul's assertion in 5:3. He says that he has been passing judgment. Secondly, it would also nullify 5:12–6:8. There he notes that judges are needed inside the church (cf. 11:13).

Paul was writing to a group of believers in the process of dividing. At the root of their divisions are matters of social and spiritual status. Again, some were associating spiritual gifts acquired in baptism with their baptizers' social and spiritual rankings. The situation was ripe for a congregational chasm. Some viewed Apollos as having higher status, some Paul, others Peter. A contingent of believers in Corinth not baptized by Paul were making snap judgments about him and speaking ill of him.

Yet, their judgments were ill-founded and arose from a misunderstanding of baptism, baptizers, spiritual gifts, and status. For three chapters now, Paul has been attempting to get them to see this. Here, in chapter 4, he drives the point home even more. Had the group in Corinth understood baptism, gifts, and the like correctly, they would have had no qualms with Paul. He hoped their hearts/motives would change.

Paul asserts that, among the faithful, a clean conscience and pure motives are important. Both merit rewards from God. Foul intentions and impure motives, however, will be exposed. Both merit punishment from God. Thus, Paul is not forbidding rightful judgment; instead, he teaches that, when believers' judgments are rooted in faulty theology, problems arise. Such persons should keep to themselves because their motives will eventually be exposed.

In a way, however, Paul is already exposing their motives. This is where judgment is misunderstood by many today. When a person does wrong, their words and/or actions are put on display before others. Yet, if a person is spiritually deaf or blind, they are incapable of recognizing that. Part of a Christian's duty is to help others see. When people can grasp the error(s) of their ways, a door has been opened by and for the gospel. This is the sin-admitting aspect of the gospel. The church must always acknowledge this; otherwise, Christ's life, death, resurrection, and ascension were in vain.

Helping others see their folly is hardly passing judgment. This is an act of loving-kindness. The motive is to see all living in shalom with God and one another. Helping someone see their sin should not be viewed as passing undue judgment. That person's words and actions have already brought judgment upon them. Instead, this is an act of proving yourself faithful to the gospel that has been entrusted to you.

1. What are the circumstances that have led some in Corinth to begin passing faulty judgment on Paul?
2. How is helping someone see the error of their ways related to judgment?

TWO

Starting to Reign

1 Corinthians 4:6–8 NET *I have applied these things to myself and Apollos because of you, brothers and sisters, so that through us you may learn "not to go beyond what is written," so that none of you will be puffed up in favor of the one against the other. ⁷For who concedes you any superiority? What do you have that you did not receive? And if you received it, why do you boast as though you did not? ⁸Already you are satisfied! Already you are rich! You have become kings without us! I wish you had become kings so that we could reign with you!*

Key Observation. True leaders take on the role of a servant, not positions on pedestals.

Understanding the Word. When most of us approach Scripture, we do so with reverence. In Scripture we expect to encounter deep wisdom, help for holy living, and God's presence. We value reading prayers, psalms, parables, and the like. When we think of engaging Scripture, the word *sarcasm* is typically not on our radars. Yet, in order to understand Paul's comments in 1 Corinthians 4:6–8, we need to have our sarcasm meters tuned up.

The apostle's sarcasm may not strike us as humorous like a modern comedian's; nevertheless, it is there. Intuitively, most of us can recognize sarcasm when we meet it. It may occur as an eye roll, shoulder shrug, or comment. We understand, for example, the sarcasm in Groucho Marx's comment, "I had a perfectly wonderful evening, but this wasn't it." So, what is "sarcasm"? It is saying one thing while implying you don't mean it. It is like saying "I promise" while crossing your fingers.

Paul's statement in 4:8 is entirely sarcastic. Paul does not really mean what he says (cf. also 4:10). He is essentially saying, "Look at you exquisite Corinthian Christians! When I was there a few months ago, you were nobodies! Perhaps

I should have stayed around a bit longer so your spiritual highness, your religious royalty, would have rubbed off on me. Boy, did I miss out!" Of course, Paul does not mean this. He does not believe that some of the believers in Corinth were nearly as esteemed as they were making themselves out to be. This is why, just a few breaths earlier, he calls them "worldly" and "infants in Christ" (3:1).

Many of the problems in Corinth, as noted, stem from misunderstanding baptism, baptizers, and gifts. Paul zeroes in on these items in 3:21–4:5. What he says here in 4:6–8 continues that train of thought. In fact, his point in 3:22–4:1, that the leaders of the congregation are all servants, is reiterated here. When Paul says, "I have applied these *things* to myself and Apollos," the *things* he is talking about are leadership and servanthood. In the church, every leader must be a servant. All the servants, despite having different roles, are social equals.

When Paul invokes the saying "Do not go beyond what is written," he is referring to that very thing. He, Apollos, Peter, and other leaders were all equal-status servants in Christ. The congregants should also view them in this light. They should see them this way instead of trying to place them on pedestals. Then they would see that their arguments and divisions are senseless and unfounded. The only way to continue pitting leaders against each another was to distort Paul's words; they must go beyond what Paul himself had written.

Many important lessons can be gleaned from these verses. One is that placing church leaders on pedestals is uncalled for and never a good idea. In a culture where celebrity pastors abound, we need to be reminded that true leaders take on the role of a servant. The church does not need any more negative PR from fame-chasing preachers who soar to great heights only to get caught up in scandal. When they fall, they also end up bringing everyone around them down. Certainly, we need to honor our leaders, but we should only do so when they are fulfilling their Christian duties as a servant first. We should be right there alongside them doing the same. And, no, I'm not being sarcastic.

1. Does it strike you as odd to find sarcasm in the Bible? Why or why not?
2. What does "Do not go beyond what is written" refer to?

THREE
Processing the Procession

1 Corinthians 4:9–13 NET *For, I think, God has exhibited us apostles last of all, as men condemned to die, because we have become a spectacle to the world, both to angels and to people. ¹⁰We are fools for Christ, but you are wise in Christ! We are weak, but you are strong! You are distinguished, we are dishonored! ¹¹To the present hour we are hungry and thirsty, poorly clothed, brutally treated, and without a roof over our heads. ¹²We do hard work, toiling with our own hands. When we are verbally abused, we respond with a blessing, when persecuted, we endure, ¹³when people lie about us, we answer in a friendly manner. We are the world's dirt and scum, even now.*

Key Observation. Cruciformity is central to the gospel.

Understanding the Word. More than a decade ago, the U.S. military came under fire upon the release of "Torture Memos" from Abu Ghraib prison. Photos leaked to the media created a storm of controversy. Guards were dragging prisoners on leashes like dogs. They were forcing inmates to disrobe and perform obscene acts on and in front of another. In many of the pictures, the American soldiers are giving a thumbs up.

The photos functioned as images of triumph. Their message was sent loud and clear: this is how we humiliate our enemies—those we view as unworthy of life. In some sense, these images resemble ancient Roman times. In today's passage, Paul alludes to such things. His remark about being "a spectacle to the world" is a reference to how Rome treated prisoners of war by placing them at the end of a victory procession.

When Rome conquered an enemy, it would parade them through town. Leaders, perhaps even the emperor, were out front showing off their spoils. Human spoils, the prisoners of war, were at the back. They were often mutilated and/or killed for entertainment's sake. If they lived, they might be imprisoned or sold into slavery. Their loss was Rome's gain. The message was clear: do not cross almighty Rome!

In the original language of the New Testament, the word "arena" is actually *theatron* (i.e., theater). In Ephesus there was a unique and magnificent theater. It is still standing today. There, prisoners' and slaves' lives came under threat. In 1 Corinthians 15:31–32, Paul says he "fought wild beasts in Ephesus" and nearly lost his life (cf. 2 Cor. 1:8–10). His contending with "beasts" was not a reference to fighting animals, but a metaphor for those persecuting him (1 Cor. 15:8–9).

In Acts 19:29, Paul says that he, Gaius, and Aristarchus rushed into the "theater" there. They were threatened by Demetrius and others (Acts 19:21–29). He and the other apostles were put on display, condemned to die, and made a spectacle. They were viewed as fools, weak, dishonored, hungry, thirsty, in rags, brutally treated, homeless, cursed, persecuted, slandered, the scum of the earth, and the garbage of the world. Now, recall that many in the congregation were arguing about status gleaned from the leader who baptized them. Paul's words undermine such views. If people were going to associate themselves with him or other apostles, they were really associating with those who have become despised scum of the earth.

Many believers in Corinth had ignored the fact that the gospel entailed suffering, that is, cruciformity. They had twisted it into a message for self-profit and self-gain. Today, perhaps nowhere more than in America, this anti-gospel has become fashionable. Motivational speakers have claimed their spots on mainstream television, garnered large followings, and lined their pockets. Many have been duped by this message of health and wealth, this twisted and heretical prosperity scheme.

When Christianity is used for self-promotion, something has gone terribly wrong. This happens not only on a large scale, but even on smaller platforms such as blogs, podcasts, YouTube channels, and the like. It is easy to locate Christian narcissism in our society. Vanity and egotism have drowned out humility. Self-righteousness has taken precedence over unity. Elitism has eradicated suffering together. As the old saying goes, "The more things change the more they stay the same."

1. What is the significance of Paul's Roman procession language and imagery in these verses? What role does it play in his overall argument?

2. What is cruciformity, and why is it imperative in the lives of Jesus's followers?

Week Three

FOUR
Like Father, like Son

1 Corinthians 4:14–17 NET *I am not writing these things to shame you, but to correct you as my dear children. ⁱ⁵For though you may have 10,000 guardians in Christ, you do not have many fathers, because I became your father in Christ Jesus through the gospel. ¹⁶I encourage you, then, be imitators of me. ¹⁷For this reason, I have sent Timothy to you, who is my dear and faithful son in the Lord. He will remind you of my ways in Christ, as I teach them everywhere in every church.*

Key Observation. There is a cost to imitating Paul, which is really an imitation of Jesus.

Understanding the Word. Christianity is not a lone-ranger religion. As the old adage says, "It takes a village!" Throughout 1 Corinthians, Paul refers to himself as apostle, brother, mother/wet nurse, planter, builder, and, among other things, servant. Here he describes himself as father. Sibling, mother/wet nurse, and father? Yes. He casts himself in virtually every household role. But was Paul out of his mind? No.

Simply put, he had different relationships with different people. Some needed a father figure, others a mother, and others an older sibling. Today, many children grow up in single-parent homes. This often forces them, at a young age, to assume mothering and fathering roles toward their siblings. The scenario in the broken household of faith at Corinth was similar.

Despite Paul's plethora of relational roles, he did not view himself as a one-man show. He was not an apostolic lone ranger. In 4:17, he tells the congregants that his pal, Timothy, would be coming along soon. Timothy was still young. Paul reminds them not to treat him with contempt (16:10). In 4:14, Paul refers to the faithful as his children. He also refers to Timothy as his child—his faithful son. Just as they should treat one another with dignity and respect, Paul urges the same toward Timothy upon arrival.

Paul's remarks are not meant to shame his letter recipients. Still, the contrast of faithful Timothy with those who have been unfaithful would have stung. Given the apostle's remarks, Timothy likely emulated Paul, especially in what he preached and taught. Thus, those who had been questioning the apostle would, when Timothy arrived, treat him similarly. Yet, Timothy would verify all Paul was saying. If Timothy's word was still not enough, they could double-check with the other congregations Paul had ministered to.

Paul's comments are, in a roundabout way, strengthening his argument. Immediately after bidding those in Corinth to imitate him, Paul holds up Timothy as Exhibit A. Timothy did just that. Paul's exhortation to imitate him is not arrogant or self-promoting. Such a reading discounts the preceding comments about being like one in a procession, one who is hungry, weak, homeless, the scum of the earth, and the garbage of the world. Paul's call is to imitate him in those things! Why? Because, within that lifestyle, there is no boasting about self, no narcissism, and no seeking fame. It is a life of sacrifice, loss, and hardship. It is a true imitation of Jesus.

Neither Jesus nor Paul considered themselves lone rangers! Jesus surrounded himself with people. He had an inner circle. First-century Christianity was collective in its makeup; it was communal to the core. In our individualism-driven society, that can be a difficult concept to grasp. Paul grieved that the unity of the community in Corinth was under threat. Cliques and individualism were taking over. Yet, he was not going to sit back, kick up his feet, and watch the congregation sink. Neither was Timothy. Neither were numerous others (see 16:10–18). They cared enough to act together so that the church might get its act together. May we do the same today!

1. When Paul tells those in Corinth to imitate him, do you think he is arrogant, overconfident, or cocky? Could a minister use such words in any setting today without being viewed with suspicion?

2. Although the apostle says that his intent is not to shame the Corinthians, do you think it is likely that when some heard this section of Paul's letter they felt ashamed? If so, who might those folks have been?

FIVE

Coming Soon

1 Corinthians 4:18–21 NET *Some have become arrogant, as if I were not coming to you. ⁱ⁹But I will come to you soon, if the Lord is willing, and I will find out not only the talk of these arrogant people, but also their power. ²⁰For the kingdom of God is demonstrated not in idle talk but with power. ²¹What do you want? Shall I come to you with a rod of discipline or with love and a spirit of gentleness?*

Key Observation. The kingdom of God is not a matter of talk but power.

Understanding the Word. In 1 Corinthians 4:18–21 it becomes clearer why Paul previously employed child-parent rhetoric. In antiquity, a father was also often the household disciplinarian. Within the household of faith, Paul took on such a role. Some of his children were being stubborn. He inquires: Do you want me to act as a disciplining father or a gentle one? Of course, it's a rhetorical question; the latter is preferable. None of them want to experience Paul the disciplinarian; thus, they should heed his "warning" (4:14).

The apostle speaks bluntly here. He says that some had become arrogant; they were boasting about themselves. Some had started rumors about Paul. Some had said he's a liar; after all, he said he was coming back, but he never had. Paul's itinerary had become a sticking point. Yet, he implies that he would indeed come again. (In fact, he did, not long after writing!) His actions would speak louder than the gossipers' words. Stated differently: the kingdom of God is not a matter of talk but power.

We must not misunderstand what is meant by this statement. Paul is not saying that preaching, evangelizing, or teaching are unimportant matters. He is also not saying that being Christian busybodies captures the essence of Christianity. Paul is saying, however, that vain talk has no place in the kingdom of God. That is, the kingdom of God has no room for gossip and slander—talk rooted in arrogance and self-aggrandizement. Such talk merely creates and reveals division. What is appropriate is that which is true and edifying: truth spoken in love and gentleness. Likewise, deeds rooted in self-sacrifice and service are appropriate. Such deeds resemble Paul's ways, which ultimately resemble Jesus's ways.

It is easy to fall into gossiping and running others into the ground, even in church settings. Today, with the advent of texting and social media, it has become even easier. It is common for folks to broadcast church-related issues for all the public to see. Churning the rumor mill and ruining someone's life takes no time. I've been on both the participating and receiving end of both. I can vouch that neither is healthy. I've had to repent of such sins and ask for forgiveness. One of my guiding principles for social media is this: do not to post anything that would cause my children or grandchildren to have shame or disappointment in me. That's a pretty good rule of thumb.

Although Paul didn't have social media to contend with, the principle behind the point remains. He wants those in Corinth to stop the shenanigans. Perhaps he didn't want them to be embarrassed down the road by what relatives from the family of faith may think. Unfortunately, for thousands of years, believers have been reading this letter, and the secret is out.

Still, we benefit from this. We can learn from such mistakes. We can do better. We can begin watching what we say and do. We can begin talking appropriately. We can begin living in powerful and edifying ways. We can discipline. We can restore gently. Standing on the shoulders of all who've gone before us, we can pave the way for the next generation of believers. We can. The question is: Will we?

1. As you read these verses aloud what tone of voice seems to fit most naturally? How might that influence your understanding of what's said here, especially about discipline?
2. What sort of talk is Paul referring to in 4:18–21? What sort of power?

WEEK THREE

GATHERING DISCUSSION OUTLINE

A. **Open session in prayer.** Ask that God would astonish us anew with fresh insight from God's Word and transform us into the disciples that Jesus desires us to become.

B. **View video for this week's readings.**

C. **Ask:** What were key insights or takeaways that you gained from your reading during the week and from watching the video commentary? In particular, how did these help you to grow in your faith and understanding of Scripture this week? What parts of the Bible lesson or study raised questions for you?

D. **Discuss questions selected from the daily readings.**

   1. **KEY OBSERVATION:** Christians are called to help others see the error of their ways.

      DISCUSSION QUESTION: How is helping someone see the error of their ways related to judgment?

   2. **KEY OBSERVATION:** True leaders take on the role of a servant, not positions on pedestals.

      DISCUSSION QUESTION: What does "Do not go beyond what is written" refer to?

3. **KEY OBSERVATION:** Cruciformity is central to the gospel.

   DISCUSSION QUESTION: What is cruciformity and why is it imperative in the lives of Jesus's followers?

4. **KEY OBSERVATION:** There is a cost to imitating Paul, which is really an imitation of Jesus.

   DISCUSSION QUESTION: When Paul tells those in Corinth to imitate him, do you think he is arrogant, overconfident, or cocky? Could a minister use such words in any setting today without being viewed with suspicion?

5. **KEY OBSERVATION:** The kingdom of God is not a matter of talk but power.

   DISCUSSION QUESTION: What sort of talk is Paul referring to in 4:18–21? What sort of power?

E. **As the study concludes, consider specific ways that this week's Bible lesson invites you to grow and calls you to change.** How do this week's scriptures call us to think differently? How do they challenge us to change in order to align ourselves with God's work in the world? What specific actions should we take to apply the insights of the lesson into our daily lives? What kind of person does our Bible lesson call us to become?

F. **Close session with prayer.** Emphasize God's ongoing work of transformation in our lives in preparation for loving mission and service in the world. Pray for absent class members as well as for persons whom we need to invite to join our study.

WEEK FOUR

1 Corinthians 5:1–13

Incest, Sex, and Church Discipline

INTRODUCTION

Galatians is likely Paul's most aggressive epistle. The apostle abstains from the standard greeting and omits thanksgiving remarks. By verse 6 he levels threats and expresses dismay. He was very frustrated when he wrote. 1 Corinthians 5:1–13 was also born out of frustration. It exudes deep disappointment.

Paul deals with sexual impropriety and misconduct within the assembly. A case of incest had become a point of division. Some were lamenting over it, while others were acting arrogant, perhaps even celebrating it. One person's actions were creating a schism. While the specific identity of the offender is not provided and remains unknown to us, everyone in the congregation there knew the culprit. Individuals were siding with him, which may suggest that he was viewed by some as a leader. Of course, many in the assembly were prone to exalting leaders.

Paul says the man should be expelled—handed over to Satan. This was to protect the congregation's unity in the Spirit. Any threat to unity in the Spirit must be excised. There is, without a doubt, a great difference between the unity itself and unity in the Spirit. It is quite possible to elevate unity to the level of an idol. It is also possible that the drive to maintain unity can become a stumbling block to maintaining unity in the Spirit.

This must have been a difficult word for the first hearers. Excommunicating someone is never easy. In today's world, it is no easier; in fact, part of me wonders if it is more difficult. Why? Because tolerance is often touted as the highest of virtues. The first sign of appearing intolerant invites social backlash. Christians who take a stand for what they believe are often labeled intolerant.

Many now view intolerance as a vice. As a result, many Christians remain quiet, back down, and fly under the radar. Many have buckled and caved in under this social pressure. Out of fear, whether knowingly or not, many Christians have allowed their understanding of intolerance to be redefined by society. Intolerance can, in fact, be very virtuous. Paul intimates as much in 1 Corinthians 5:1–13: having intolerance toward sins such as sexual immorality, greed, swindling, idolatry, and getting drunk is virtuous.

What we need to recover is a Pauline view of intolerance, a healthy view where sin is not tolerated. That may be easier said than done, especially in a context where churches are prone today to baptizing sin and calling it good and holy. But, for those of us who know better, may we not tolerate such things. May we realize that sin threatens unity in the Spirit and, therefore, must be expelled.

ONE
The Trading Bunch

1 Corinthians 5:1–2 NLT *I can hardly believe the report about the sexual immorality going on among you—something that even pagans don't do. I am told that a man in your church is living in sin with his stepmother. ²You are so proud of yourselves, but you should be mourning in sorrow and shame. And you should remove this man from your fellowship.*

Key Observation. We must be careful not to make an idol of unity.

Understanding the Word. American culture is sex-crazed; its sex drive is insatiable. It may well be that no society, at any time in history, has been as obsessed with sex/sexuality. Considering ancient Greece's history, that's saying something! Every form of media today has been co-opted by a hypersexual agenda. Unsurprisingly, rampant sexual promiscuity, human trafficking, and the child sex trade are also larger than ever.

Church leaders struggle to articulate a sexual ethic consistent with the teachings of Scripture. The progressive perspective, parading the evolution of intellectual growth and sophistication, promotes a new understanding about sexual matters.

Paul makes it clear that sexual aberrations are serious matters. They may merit church discipline, even expulsion. Paul's brand of progressive meant adhering to church discipline. Focusing on sexuality while conveniently ignoring discipline and expulsion is little more than an act of recreating Paul in one's own marred, progressive image.

Paul noted that he has heard about sexual immorality in the church. Paul used a Greek term whose root is "porn" (from which we also get "*forn*icator"). In this instance, a son was sleeping with his father's wife. He was engaging in incest with his stepmom. Evidently, some were proud of the lad. Paul said such things do not even occur among the pagans/Gentiles. How, then, could it be permitted in a church setting?

Paul did not dismiss it as a minor matter. Instead, his response was: "I'm disappointed. You all should have broken fellowship with this man!" Today, entire denominations are threatened by wayward leaders adopting modern-day sexual ethics, attempting to graft them into the church. Instead of following Paul's lead, they suggested that they know better. Instead of breaking fellowship with sinners, they adopted their practices and call them good and holy.

Yet, even amid a letter about overcoming threats to unity, Paul was not a slave to it. He was not willing to call sin holy in order to preserve it. Unity was important to Paul, but he never made it an idol! For Paul, the only way to really, truly preserve unity (in the Spirit), was to eradicate the sin within that threatens it.

Who will confront sin, call it what it is, and treat it how it should be treated? Who will do this to preserve unity among God's people? Who will help the church keep her house in order regarding sex-related matters? Who is willing to break ties with those whose sin threatens true fellowship? Who will stand up and speak up?

1. Paul wrote 1 Corinthians in large part to help the congregants overcome threats to unity. Instead of calling divisive persons and actions good and holy, he believed that expelling them was what would truly create unity. Should the church of today adopt such practices?

2. Where, in Paul's view, are those within the church supposed to draw a line with those who self-identify as believers yet engage in sinful living?

TWO
Over and Out

1 Corinthians 5:3–5 NLT *Even though I am not with you in person, I am with you in the Spirit. And as though I were there, I have already passed judgment on this man ⁴in the name of the Lord Jesus. You must call a meeting of the church. I will be present with you in spirit, and so will the power of our Lord Jesus. ⁵Then you must throw this man out and hand him over to Satan so that his sinful nature will be destroyed and he himself will be saved on the day the Lord returns.*

Key Observation. When the Spirit is absent, the church ceases to be herself.

Understanding the Word. Years ago, I saw a first-person monologue where the actor played C. S. Lewis. The show was brilliant. At times, I forgot I was not watching Lewis himself. The actor's voice, mannerisms, and stories were so realistic, it was as if Clive Staples himself was there. In some sense, Paul hoped that 1 Corinthians would have a similar function.

This letter would not have been passed around and read quietly by individuals. It would have been read aloud before the community. Even more, Paul would have coached the letter-carrier, also the presenter-performer, on how best to perform it. The end goal: to lead the hearers to feel as though Paul himself was there speaking. Although not physically present, he was present in spirit. Via a performer, his epistolary presence was made known.

Some may have blamed Paul for the incestuous man's deeds. He was culpable in the man's sin, they argued, because he hadn't taught them clearly about the Law. They thought he had shunned the Law. Thus, the commands against incest no longer applied. Yet, even in Roman law, incest was forbidden. Paul, a Roman citizen, was disgusted at such actions. Paul laid the foundations for ethics and theology in all the churches he started (see 1 Cor. 3:10–12; 7:17, 19).

The apostle told the assemblers in Corinth to expel the incestuous man and hand him (i.e., his flesh) over to Satan. The "Satan" figure is neither a Roman official nor a person in general (i.e., an accuser). This is Satan, the enemy of

God. Such a command, undoubtedly, seems harsh to modern sensitivities. In congregations where political correctness reigns and offending someone runs the risk of losing them (and their money!), this is a bold word.

This man was to be handed over so that the Spirit would be preserved among the believers on the day of the Lord. Paul was looking ahead to Christ's return but was also concerned with the present. Expelling and handing over is a means of removing sin and preventing division. Where sin is offered a home to dwell, there is no room for the Spirit abide. Paul was not merely writing to preserve the unity of the assembly, but to preserve the presence of the Spirit. The Spirit is the glue that unifies the assembly.

Again, Paul never elevated unity to the status of an idol. Paul wrote so those in Corinth would be aware of the Spirit's presence. Anything threatening the Spirit's presence is cause for removal. When the Spirit is absent, the church ceases to be herself. But what causes the Spirit to leave? Blasphemy: attaching that which is vain to that which is holy. The incestuous man mixed vain sexual practices with a holy act (i.e., sex). Others attempted mixing the presence of sin, manifest in the incestuous man, with the presence of the Holy Spirit. But the two simply cannot coexist; a house divided falls (Matt. 12:25). Unless the sinner is expelled, there is no room for the Holy Spirit.

One might respond: We're all sinners, does that mean there is not room for us? Well, once one becomes a believer, they no longer view themselves as a sinner. "Sin remains," as Wesley said, "but no longer reigns."* We are called to sanctification. We no longer view ourselves as sinners. We strive to avoid sin. When it happens, we cut it off immediately. When we do, we move on toward maturity and perfection in Christ.

1. How is the presence of the Spirit related to the unity of believers?
2. Why is the presence of sin, especially blasphemy, a threat to the presence of the Spirit? How?

---

*https://www.ccel.org/ccel/wesley/sermons.v.xiii.html.

THREE
Out with the Old, in with the New

1 Corinthians 5:6–8 NLT *Your boasting about this is terrible. Don't you realize that this sin is like a little yeast that spreads through the whole batch of dough? ⁷Get rid of the old "yeast" by removing this wicked person from among you. Then you will be like a fresh batch of dough made without yeast, which is what you really are. Christ, our Passover Lamb, has been sacrificed for us. ⁸So let us celebrate the festival, not with the old bread of wickedness and evil, but with the new bread of sincerity and truth.*

Key Observation. That which is holy cannot be mixed with that which is vain.

Understanding the Word. Everyone has a backstory. It consists of certain people, places, and events. It has its own shape and contour. Part of my story: I became a Christian just before my senior year of high school. A specific chain of events occurred, which led me to attend a Christian university. My experiences there led me to do my Masters of Divinity. It was a rather liberal seminary, and I was the only evangelical there. This forced me to articulate my beliefs with newfound clarity and sophistication. The notion of being a Bible scholar emerged for the first time.

These details are quite general. Still, they provide some idea of the early stages of my faith journey. Had I not told you, you would have less understanding about my background and me. Paul has a backstory too. Details are embedded in his letters. Some have to do with his ancient Jewish heritage. His remarks, for instance, about leavened and unleavened bread, are indicators of that. In Judaism there were numerous feast days. One was the Feast of Unleavened Bread. Another was Passover. Paul used words that allude to both.

Passover derives from Exodus. It commemorates God's deliverance of Israel from Egypt. When Israel crossed into the promised land, the people celebrated this. One of the first things they ate was unleavened bread (Josh. 5:11–12). The Feast of Unleavened Bread was connected to the exodus. It denoted how Israel left Egypt with haste. There was not time for the bread to leaven. Part of Paul's own background has echoes of exile and deliverance.

This image arises amid an exhortation concerning expulsion. The incestuous man having sex with his stepmother must be expelled. In antiquity, as today, breadmaking consisted of mixing water, flour, and yeast. This process was known as leavening. The result was a loaf of bread. Old or dead yeast ruins a loaf, making it flat and tasteless. New or fresh yeast yielded an optimal loaf. Yeast is a leavening agent.

Symbolically, old yeast is represented by arrogance, malice, and wickedness. It cannot be mixed in with the church. The result will be ruin. New yeast, represented by sincerity and truth, yields the desired result—unity via the Spirit in the body of Christ (10:16). In short: that which is holy cannot be mixed with that which is vain.

Paul told those in Corinth to expel the man. Why? In order that the Spirit would preserve unity among them. They must get rid of the old yeast (i.e., the incestuous man and sexual immorality) because if one tries to mix it with the new yeast, it will ruin it. Old yeast cannot be mixed with the new work (i.e., renewing work) of the Spirit of Christ. Old yeast cannot foster an atmosphere for the Spirit to dwell in and work afresh. If the congregation in Corinth wishes to protect itself, it will need to rise up (pun intended!) and do what's right. It must put the Spirit in the foreground of its story.

1. In what ways does Paul's yeast metaphor connect to his preceding comments about expelling the wicked man from the assembly?

2. How does Paul's background along with things occurring in the Corinthian assembly shape the language and imagery he uses here?

FOUR
Guilty by Association

1 Corinthians 5:9–10 NLT *When I wrote to you before, I told you not to associate with people who indulge in sexual sin. ¹⁰But I wasn't talking about unbelievers who indulge in sexual sin, or are greedy, or cheat people, or worship idols. You would have to leave this world to avoid people like that.*

Key Observation. Christians ought to wage war on sin.

Understanding the Word. My family tree has few writers. It's a long line of blue-collar workers. My grandpa, affectionately known as "Smitty," died when I was eleven. He was a steely truck driver. I recently learned, nearly twenty years after the fact, that when he died his company created an annual award in his name. He was known by his colleagues as a hard worker and innovator.

I have vivid memories of him in his sixties. He was confined to a hospice bed in the back of his mobile home. I took him breakfast in the mornings along with a medicinal milkshake. When he died, I learned that he was a Christian. I also discovered that he was a poet. He kept small books of original poems written while on the road. They were stowed away in his bedroom closet. I have inherited these treasured possessions. One poem is titled "Our All-Out Fight." It reminds me, in some ways, of 1 Corinthians 5:9–10. It says:

> The only way to victory / Toward our everlasting goal,
> Is that good character which is / The wisdom of the soul.
>
> The wisdom of obedience / However sad our plight,
> With never any compromise / Between the wrong and right.
>
> No partial courage will suffice / Upon the battle scene,
> There is no half-way method or / A sort of "in-between."
>
> In weakness we may stumble and / Eventually fall down,
> But we must rise and fight again / If we would win our crown.
>
> Our weakness is a heritage / But never an excuse,
> To end the war we wage on sin / Or make the shortest truce.

My grandpa was right! Christians ought to wage war on sin. Followers of Christ should never make a truce with sin. They should avoid sin and expel it.

He (re)commanded members of the body of Christ to not associate with those fostering sin. He specifically mentioned sexual immorality, greed, swindling, and idolatry. He placed emphasis on not associating with those "inside" the assembly acting like believers but doing such things. He called for judgment by and upon those inside. There was a distinct focus on in-house affairs. As for those outside, no judgment needed—that would be futile. The gospel should be shared with them.

The believers in Corinth, after all, came to Christ through evangelism, not judgment. That's what Paul was getting at when he said, "In that case you would have to leave this world." Judgment cannot precede evangelism. Preaching the gospel helps folks see their sinful ways. Then the Holy Spirit convicts and persuades people while leading them into truth.

Remember the "Two Ways" tradition? It is present here too. Paul said that those in Corinth chose to step out of the worldly realm and into the spiritual realm. They did so by hearing the gospel and following the lead of the Spirit. They no longer walk in the worldly realm. They have a new identity. They are new leaven. If they want to step out of their identity in Christ to be someone less than God desires, they will become old leaven. Thus, they must stand firm amid the "All-Out Fight" against sin they find themselves in.

1. If there is another allusion to the "Two Ways" tradition here, why do you think Paul might have referred to it?
2. Why are Christians called to judge those inside but not those outside?

FIVE

It's What's on the Inside

1 Corinthians 5:11–13 NLT *I meant that you are not to associate with anyone who claims to be a believer yet indulges in sexual sin, or is greedy, or worships idols, or is abusive, or is a drunkard, or cheats people. Don't even eat with such people.*

¹²It isn't my responsibility to judge outsiders, but it certainly is your responsibility to judge those inside the church who are sinning. ¹³God will judge those on the outside; but as the Scriptures say, "You must remove the evil person from among you."

Key Observation. When Christians judge outsiders, it is an encroachment on God's territory and sovereignty.

Understanding the Word. In 2013, Edward Snowden became a household name overnight. Snowden, having worked for the U.S. government, leaked nearly two million files to the public. The files contained sensitive information.

After fleeing for his life, Snowden received sanctuary in Russia. Many deem him a turncoat and traitor. To them, he took advantage of the in-group trust placed in him. He acted opportunistically. Thus, government officials sought to banish him and protect their identity.

One's identity tells who they are and what they are about. There are, of course, false identities, too, especially on social media. In the U.S., where many are confused about sexuality, gender, ethnicity, and the like, identity problems abound. This makes navigating the world a challenge. A healthy sense of identity, however, helps.

When I meet believers for the first time, there's often an immediate connection. Why? We have a shared identity. Our ethics, goals, and thought processes are rooted in Christ. This sense of connection creates a tight bond in a brief span of time. When Paul uses kinship language, something similar occurs. It creates a bond, and he wants to protect it. He desires that for all his congregations. If it means banishing or expelling someone in order to preserve unity brought about by the Spirit, that's okay. Paul had other things in mind too: (1) Christians should engage in judging within the church, particularly among Christians; (2) believers should not judge those outside the church; and (3) Paul did not desire a theocracy.

Concerning the first two points, congregants should be concerned with in-house affairs rather than outside ones. Attempting to use Christian values and beliefs to judge those outside the assembly is futile. They have not submitted to the gospel and have no commitment to it. It is like having a baseball umpire judge a football game—it doesn't work. On the third point, instituting a theocracy and forcing people to abide by our ways is wrong. It prevents hearers of the gospel from having the opportunity to be persuaded by it. It also prevents an honest pledge of allegiance.

Helping people make that pledge is the work of the Holy Spirit. Christians should never force their belief on others. A gospel void of human choice is no gospel at all. To make a choice is to make a judgment. Christians are called to judge and make judgments. The sad trope that "Christians are called to love, not judge" is not true. Christians judge out of love.

Thus, when individuals within the church are sexually immoral, greedy, swindling, idolatrous, and drunkards, believers are called to judge them. If they continue sinning, they should be expelled. Paul commanded believers in

Corinth not to eat with the unrepentant who identify as believers. This could be a reference to Communion. It could mean sharing a meal in general. As we shall see later, food matters will become a focal point.

If a believer engaging in sin repents, they are welcome to stay. As for non-believers, God will judge them. That is his duty. Christians judging outsiders is an encroachment on God's territory and sovereignty. It is an attempt to usurp his authority. It is losing sight of their identity. Today's church desperately needs to hear this.

1. Why is it important to recognize that the apostle sanctions judging within the body of Christ but not outside it?

2. What does it suggest about the nature and character of God that he will judge those outside the body of Christ? And what does it suggest about his nature and character that he affords believers the ability to judge one another within the assembly?

WEEK FOUR

GATHERING DISCUSSION OUTLINE

A. **Open session in prayer**. Ask that God would astonish us anew with fresh insight from God's Word and transform us into the disciples that Jesus desires us to become.

B. **View video for this week's readings.**

C. **Ask:** What were key insights or takeaways that you gained from your reading during the week and from watching the video commentary? In particular, how did these help you to grow in your faith and understanding of Scripture this week? What parts of the Bible lesson or study raised questions for you?

D. **Discuss questions selected from the daily readings.**

   1. **KEY OBSERVATION:** We must be careful not to make an idol of unity.

      DISCUSSION QUESTION: Paul wrote 1 Corinthians in large part to help the congregants overcome threats to unity. Instead of calling divisive persons and actions good and holy, he believed that expelling them was what would truly create unity. Should the church of today adopt such practices?

   2. **KEY OBSERVATION:** When the Spirit is absent, the church ceases to be herself.

      DISCUSSION QUESTION: Why is the presence of sin, especially blasphemy, a threat to the presence of the Spirit? How?

3. **KEY OBSERVATION:** That which is holy cannot be mixed with that which is vain.

   DISCUSSION QUESTION: In what ways does Paul's yeast metaphor connect to his preceding comments about expelling the wicked man from the assembly?

4. **KEY OBSERVATION:** Christians ought to wage war on sin.

   DISCUSSION QUESTION: Why are Christians called to judge those inside but not those outside?

5. **KEY OBSERVATION:** When Christians judge outsiders, it is an encroachment on God's territory and sovereignty.

   DISCUSSION QUESTION: What does it suggest about the nature and character of God that he will judge those outside the body of Christ? And what does it suggest about his nature and character that he affords believers the ability to judge one another within the assembly?

E. **As the study concludes, consider specific ways that this week's Bible lesson invites you to grow and calls you to change.** How do this week's scriptures call us to think differently? How do they challenge us to change in order to align ourselves with God's work in the world? What specific actions should we take to apply the insights of the lesson into our daily lives? What kind of person does our Bible lesson call us to become?

F. **Close session with prayer.** Emphasize God's ongoing work of transformation in our lives in preparation for loving mission and service in the world. Pray for absent class members as well as for persons whom we need to invite to join our study.

WEEK FIVE

1 Corinthians 6:1–20

Judges, Swindlers, and the Sexually Immoral

INTRODUCTION

In 2015 a song titled "Lips Are Movin" by Meghan Trainor hit the airwaves. It was up-tempo and happy. Even so, in the hook of the song the singer claimed she knew the person was lying because his lips were moving. The singer is the one cheated on. Despite being upbeat, it is ultimately a song about infidelity and the resultant pain. The rhythm and bubbly nature of the song cause listeners to miss or overlook this. In fact, the song may even put a listener in a good mood. It's like watching a movie and suddenly realizing you've been tricked into empathizing with and rooting for the villain.

This is a good example of how prevalent sexual immorality, even in the form of infidelity, is in our culture. It has become so commonplace that we hardly realize it. In fact, we sing right along without realizing it. As we do, such things become ingrained in us, and we become desensitized. As followers of Jesus, however, we must not succumb to sin, especially sexual sin. Such matters are very serious. As we read Paul's epistle, we are privileged to see how he understands, thinks through, and speaks about the matter. In 1 Corinthians 6 we realize that his standards for sexual ethics are built upon the foundation of Jesus's resurrection. When one steps off that foundation, things get shaky and dangerous. Likewise, stepping off the foundation threatens unity in the Spirit.

Paul was concerned about his brothers and sisters in Corinth. At times, it seems he was throwing himself in front of a runaway train in hopes of averting danger ahead. In his absence, he urged believers to appoint leaders to render judgments about important matters. They would also help maintain the unity of the Spirit. Sin poses a real threat. Paul did not beat around the bush or sugarcoat things; he said what he meant and meant what he said.

The apostle was painfully aware of the fact that the worldly realm can desensitize God's people. That realm is filled with and catered to liars, swindlers, and the sexually immoral. He was also aware that, if one walks in the spiritual realm, they can overcome. Christians should not sing along to the tune of the world; they have their own song. The lyrics focus on holiness, sanctification, and redemption. And that's no lie.

ONE
Been There, Done That!

1 Corinthians 6:1–4 NRSV *When any of you has a grievance against another, do you dare to take it to court before the unrighteous, instead of taking it before the saints? ²Do you not know that the saints will judge the world? And if the world is to be judged by you, are you incompetent to try trivial cases? ³Do you not know that we are to judge angels—to say nothing of ordinary matters? ⁴If you have ordinary cases, then, do you appoint as judges those who have no standing in the church?*

Key Observation. Judgment rooted in Christian convictions should yield godly justice.

Understanding the Word. The Latin phrase "*Veni, Vidi, Vici*" means "I came, I saw, I conquered." Its English cousin may well be "Been there, done that!" When I read 1 Corinthians 6:1–4 (as well as 6:5–8), I hear a similar sentiment. In terms of dealing with law, Paul had been there and done that. He had firsthand experience. He had wisdom to share. He knew about legal systems in general, but the Corinthian legal system in particular.

Consider Acts 18:1–18. Luke recounted events that occurred while Paul was in Corinth in the early 50s, most notably his trial before Gallio. He was charged by a group of Jews with persuading people to worship God in ways contrary to the Law. The Achaian Proconsul responded, saying, "If you Jews made complained about some misdemeanor or serious crime, I would listen.

You, however, have questions about words and names related to your own law. Settle the matter yourselves. I will not judge such things" (vv. 14–15).

Following that, the religious officials beat Sosthenes, a synagogue leader. Gallio showed no concern. This reveals that: (1) The synagogue had its own customs and laws; and (2) governmental officials did not judge daily or petty cases with no bearing on secular matters. These shaped Paul's own thinking about making judgments among believers in Corinth.

Paul knew, however, that there were some level-headed individuals in the church. He insisted that they should be appointed, as in the synagogue, to settle disputes. He himself had experienced in-house affairs, usually religious with no bearing on major legal matters, brought before governmental officials. They simply didn't care. Even more, believers ended up looking petty and foolish in front of them. To outsiders it suggested that the Christian brothers and sisters were not really a family after all; they could not trust one another.

While the congregation could protect itself from shame by avoiding taking matters before non-believing judges, the bigger takeaway was this: whereas outside authorities did not care about what happened among God's people, those inside should. It meant nothing to outside judges that believers were bickering over spiritual gifts. Yet, it meant everything to Paul and the congregation.

Judgment rooted in Christian convictions should yield godly justice. Secular judgments from non-believers are void of such convictions. Paul urged the believers in Corinth to set up a system of judgment. Once again, then, Christians are called to judge. The apostle employs a greater-to-lesser form of logic. He contended that, in the future, believers would assist God in rendering judgment (see 1 Cor. 5:13). Thus, the logic is: if you will participate in grand judgments in the future, you should be capable of participating in simple, daily judgments now. Perhaps only some were actually mature enough at the time of writing to do such things.

We see another reference to Paul's Two Realms theology here. The ways of the world are scorned by those in the church. Walking in the Spirit, that is, in the spiritual realm, is the only true option. Paul's thinking is summed up in the following maxim: "Scorn the world now and judge it later; judge the saints now and preserve the Spirit among them so that they shall be saved later." Of such a thing, no one can yet say, "Been there, done that!"

1. How does the passage in Acts 18 potentially shed light on what Paul says in 1 Corinthians 6:1–4?
2. What are some reasons Paul preferred for Christians to do their judging in-house rather than taking matters outside?

TWO

Family Feud

1 Corinthians 6:5–8 NRSV *I say this to your shame. Can it be that there is no one among you wise enough to decide between one believer and another, ⁶but a believer goes to court against a believer—and before unbelievers at that?*

⁷In fact, to have lawsuits at all with one another is already a defeat for you. Why not rather be wronged? Why not rather be defrauded? ⁸But you yourselves wrong and defraud—and believers at that.

Key Observation. The church is not a shop of secrets, but a house of honesty.

Understanding the Word. Dealing with family isn't always easy. Feuds are inevitable. The old saying "We hurt those we love the most" is something of an absolute. Those we spend the most time with, love the most, invest the most in, and trust the most are often the ones we hurt the worst. Likewise, they are often the same people who hurt us. Family dynamics can be tricky to navigate.

A healthy family can be very life-giving. A home built on trust, commitment, love, and fidelity is the best kind of home. Throughout 1 Corinthians, Paul used kinship terminology. He longed to draw believers together, to remind them that their faith bond superseded even their blood bond. Many in the assembly at Corinth lacked the maturity to grasp that truth. They bragged, argued, and divided. Therefore, Paul, inhabiting a culture built on honor and shame, told his siblings that what he was saying was meant to shame them. He was disappointed in his brothers and sisters, and he wanted them to know it.

This dynamic helps us make sense of this entire section. Paul hoped that the congregation would appoint in-house leaders to handle disputes among believers. Paul asked if such persons exist, expecting an answer in the affirmative. They should have already done this. That failure is reason enough to be shamed by Paul. That is only compounded by the shame they've brought upon themselves by taking disputes into public and before outsiders.

In 1 Corinthians 5:7, Paul went as far as to say that the congregants in Corinth had been completely defeated in this way. Paul, of course, was not trying to muzzle people or cover over the truth. Exposing corruption in the church wasn't the topic at hand. Paul was talking about settling disagreements. Again, situating it within the honor-shame paradigm helps clarify that. Instead, the point is: wronging and cheating one another signals in-house defeat. The standard context for dealing with cheating and wronging and settling disputes was the public court system.

Paul desired a strict system of judgment within the church for such matters. The judges should be individuals with resurrection-tinted lenses. Under this type of system, in-house judgments would be made fairly and equitably. The result would not be complete defeat, but complete unity in the Spirit. Paul's question, then, is really, "Would you rather be completely defeated or lose a little public honor?" Put differently, Paul was asking, "Would you rather be completely defeated as a congregation and win a little public honor via a court victory or lose a little honor by not taking a sibling in the faith to public court and beating them?" Winning court cases in Corinth, a lawyer-saturated city, was a means of gaining social prestige and honor. Paul had no interest in such things.

He preferred honest and equitable judgments within the church. A favorable judgment there would not result in public honor; it wasn't about that. Instead, Christian judgments are about achieving unity in the Spirit. That may even mean expelling sometimes and forgiving while moving forward together other times.

Recently, a so-called Christian celebrity was found guilty of molesting his younger sisters. The family thought, however, that it was better for victims to "take one for the team" and protect their church's image. In such a case, however, the family should have come forward, exposed the sin, and held the perpetrator accountable. Paul would have applauded that! The church is not a shop of secrets, but a house of honesty.

1. Do you think the maxim "We hurt those we love the most" is true? Why or why not?

2. What are some positive reasons for having a system of judgment in place within the church?

THREE
A Good Heir Day

1 Corinthians 6:9–11 *Or do you not know that wrongdoers will not inherit the kingdom of God? Do not be deceived: Neither the sexually immoral nor idolaters nor adulterers nor men who [receive homosexual acts nor men who give homosexual acts]* ¹⁰*nor thieves nor the greedy nor drunkards nor slanderers nor swindlers will inherit the kingdom of God.* ¹¹*And that is what some of you were. But you were washed, you were sanctified, you were justified in the name of the Lord Jesus Christ and by the Spirit of our God.*

Key Observations. Allegiance to King Jesus provides freedom in God's presence here and now.

Understanding the Word. Of the 437 verses in 1 Corinthians, the three in today's reading may be referenced more than any others in American society. Why? A couple terms found in 1 Corinthians 6:9 relate to homosexuality. We need to consider these terms. If we transliterate (not translate!), that is, give a letter-for-letter equivalent from Greek to English, the words are *malakōs* and *arsenōkoitēs*. The latter, arsenōkoitēs, is a Greek compound word. *Arsēn*, which means "male," is joined with *koitē*, which means "bed" or "couch." The image is one man taking another man to bed and performing same-sex acts upon him. Paul borrows this from Leviticus 18:22 and/or 20:13.

In Hebrew the same idea is implied. *Zachar*, which means "male," is combined with *mishkav*, which means "couch," "bed," or a "place to lie down." The terminology has in view a male who takes another male to bed for the purpose of gratifying his own sexual desires. This would typically entail anal penetration. This is worth noting because arsenōkoitēs and malakōs denote different ideas. Whereas an arsenōkoitēs is the giver of a same-sex act, a malakōs is the receiver. (Note: A malakōs was not, as some have suggested, a catamite—a young boy kept by an adult for homosexual gratification. Likewise, Paul was not talking about prostitution, whether in the temple, or elsewhere here. He had specific terms he used for such words elsewhere.)

Discussions of same-sex activity dominate these verses. As a result, some aspects have been overlooked. Paul's comments focused on those who will and will not inherent God's kingdom. He listed numerous sins, "unrighteous" deeds, saying they prevent persons from being God's heirs. He issued an imperative that believers neither be deceived nor led astray.

The language of inheritance is kinship language. An inheritance was typically issued upon the death of a father. This heir language also seems to denote royalty. A king, during his reign, would strive to produce heirs so the kingdom could live on and flourish. Thus, being an heir was not simply a status recognized after a king's death, but also while living. A royal heir had present and future benefits.

When Paul said the unrighteous will not be heirs of God's kingdom, he meant now and later. Those engaging in sin brought wrath, that is, God's absence, upon themselves. Those who flee from sin, however, become washed, sanctified, and justified. They began experiencing their inheritance—freedom in God's presence—now. The opposite of God's wrath/absence is his presence. To be justified means to receive a "not guilty" verdict in God's presence. A justified person has been forgiven and accepted by God; they have experienced God's justifying grace and holy presence.

God's sanctifying grace, as noted in 1 Corinthians 1:2, has to do with the disposition or posture of one's heart toward God, others, self, and creation. Entire sanctification is the first repositioning of our heart so we can love purely. By it we overcome original sin. It is followed by progressive sanctification, a process in which the heart is repeatedly nudged back into position on the path to overcoming personal sin. In this way we move nearer to God, the epicenter of holiness, and become holy just as he is holy. Every king, after all, wants his heirs to follow his lead, to be like him, to share his goals and aspirations, to do as he does, to speak as he speaks, and in a nutshell, to have the mind he has (1 Cor. 2:16).

1. What does it mean to be an heir of God's kingdom?
2. What is the significance of believers realizing that they are heirs of God's kingdom in the present *and* the future rather than in the future only?

FOUR

The Body Politic

1 Corinthians 6:12–14 *[You say] "I have the right to do anything" . . . [I say]—but not everything is beneficial. [You say] "I have the right to do anything"—[I say] but, I will not be mastered by anything.* ¹³*You say, "Food for the stomach and the stomach for food, and God will destroy them both." [I say] The body, however, is not meant for sexual immorality but for the Lord, and the Lord for the body.* ¹⁴*By his power God raised the Lord from the dead, and he will raise us also.*

Key Observation. The resurrection should form the basis of how we think about and treat the body—and not just our own either.

Understanding the Word. I love words, wordplay, jokes, puns, jingles, catchphrases, and slogans. I am intrigued by the process behind the creation of a good one-liner. I am fascinated by sticky slogans: "You're in good hands."; "Just Do It!"; "I'm lovin' it!"; "Don't Leave Home Without It!" Slogans surround us. In Paul's day, ads and figures of speech were common too. In 1 Corinthians 6:12–14 we see three mottos used by a contingent of Corinthian believers. Paul offered a rebuttal to each.

When some said they had the freedom to do anything, Paul said not everything is beneficial. The vices listed in 6:9–11 are likely in view: sexual immorality, idolatry, adultery, receiving same-sex acts, giving same-sex acts, stealing, being drunk, being greedy, slandering, and swindling. Anyone is free to do such things, but they are not beneficial. Sin is never beneficial because it is treason against God. It violates others and self. It creates alienation in relationships. Paul, however, says he will not be mastered by anything.

Taking freedom to the extreme enslaves one to it. Drug use is a good example. Years ago, someone close to me was introduced to heroin. One use hooked them. It destroyed their life in so many ways. They lost their children and spent time in both jail and rehab. The freedom to use heroin led to a state of being taken captive by it. All sin functions this way.

The third slogan Paul refuted leads to his main point. Some of the Corinthians were heralding a food-related statement. They were suggesting that, eventually, the body would be destroyed, therefore, what we eat or do to it now, does not matter. For the apostle, however, the body absolutely mattered. The resurrection should form the basis of how we think about and treat the body—and not just our own either. That God raised Jesus's body proves that. The logic is: (1) God raised Jesus's body from the dead; therefore, our bodies matter to God; (2) if our bodies matter to God, they should also matter to us; (3) if my body matters to me (because it matters to God), and if God cares about others' bodies, then I should also care about others' bodies; (4) this means that I should live in a way that cares for and respects my own body as well as others' bodies; and (5) how I treat my body in this life is a means of preparing it for the next one. The same principle holds for how I treat others' bodies (as well as the whole of creation).

This Christian ethic, rooted in the resurrection, sets the standard for how to treat others and ourselves. Sins against the body (ours or others') are grave sins (see 1 Corinthians 6:18 and 11:27). Thus, killing, slavery, sexual sins, murder, suicide, mistreating the body, obesity, abusing others, exploiting others, etc., are all very serious sins. These sins are, at their core, anti-resurrection because they war against the body.

For Paul, the resurrection functions as the central theological tenet that can unite those in Corinth. All their thinking, feeling, and speaking should flow from belief about the resurrection. If they get this right, they will find unity in the Spirit. Once those in Corinth see everything through the lens of the resurrection, they will see how it relates to their everyday lives. Once they're at that point, they'll be able to say of the body, "I'm lovin' it!"

1. Why is treating our bodies and others' bodies in holy ways so important?

2. How might a negative or careless view of the body affect how one lives?

FIVE
Best Buy

1 Corinthians 6:15–20 NRSV *Do you not know that your bodies are members of Christ? Should I therefore take the members of Christ and make them members of a prostitute? Never! [16]Do you not know that whoever is united to a prostitute becomes one body with her? For it is said, "The two shall be one flesh." [17]But anyone united to the Lord becomes one spirit with him. [18]Shun fornication! [You say], "Every sin that a person commits is outside the body." [I say] But the fornicator sins against the body itself. [19]Or do you not know that your body is a temple of the Holy Spirit within you, which you have from God, and that you are not your own? [20]For you were bought with a price; therefore, glorify God in your body.*

Key Observation. The price at which Jesus bought his people was steep.

Understanding the Word. About 25 percent of the verses in 1 Corinthians contain questions. That's 1 out of every 4 verses. If one examines every place Paul asked a question, they will see a pattern emerge, namely, question stacking. Paul rarely asked a single question. He liked asking multiple questions in succession. In 1 Corinthians 6, nearly 60 percent of the verses contain questions. In 1 Corinthians 6:15–20, Paul asked four rhetorical questions. Thus, he wasted no time waiting for responses. He answered them himself.

Paul's interrogatives cover the themes of sexuality and the body. An intriguing feature of these verses is the frequent play on words. He said believers should never unite their bodies with a prostitute. Could this be a reference to the stepson and stepmother in 5:1–13? That is unlikely; that passage focused on incest. In 1 Corinthians 6 Paul mentioned sexual sins in general, but in 1 Corinthians 5 specific people were in view. Further, the questions asked here are plural, denoting a group.

When reading 6:15, we must remember that prostitutes received wages for engaging in sexual activities. (Paul was aware of sexual immorality in general as well as in particular.) His statement about engaging a prostitute is shocking because he contrasted it with the work of Jesus. In 6:20 he reminded the believers that *they* were bought at/with a price. A prostitute is bought to temporarily gratify the body's sexual urges. Jesus, however, bought people that they might honor God with their bodies.

We also hear an echo of redemption, which was mentioned in 1:30. It is a term borrowed from the marketplace, a payment necessary to fulfill a debt. The price at which Jesus bought his people was steep. The price to buy a prostitute, not so much. Additionally, whereas the latter divides us from truly knowing ourselves, the other, and God more closely, the former certainly doesn't. Believers are not to unite with prostitutes but to unite with Christ through his redeeming work via the Holy Spirit.

There is also an echo of Genesis (2:24) as well as Jesus's teachings (Matt. 19:5; Mark 10:7) here. Sex should only occur between one couple—a husband (biological male) and a wife (biological female). Sex outside this is a perversion God's intentions. Here, Paul quoted another Corinthian slogan: "[You say] All sins a person commits are outside the body." It's the opposite that's true—all sexual sins are sins against the body.

Just as God's Spirit inhabited the temple, after the resurrection of Jesus and the sending of the Spirit, the Spirit now inhabits God's people. Believers are both a person and a residence. It is not beyond possibility, however, that the Spirit might evacuate the premises under the right (or wrong!) circumstances. Thus, Paul urged those in Corinth to do what's right. Their bodies, which make up the body of Christ, are the locale of the Spirit. That is something they cannot put a price or number on!

1. What does it suggest about God that he bought us at a price? What does it suggest about us?

2. How do we know that God cares what we do to our own bodies as well as others' bodies? Why does it matter?

WEEK FIVE

GATHERING DISCUSSION OUTLINE

A. **Open session in prayer.** Ask that God would astonish us anew with fresh insight from God's Word and transform us into the disciples that Jesus desires us to become.

B. **View video for this week's readings.**

C. **Ask:** What were key insights or takeaways that you gained from your reading during the week and from watching the video commentary? In particular, how did these help you to grow in your faith and understanding of Scripture this week? What parts of the Bible lesson or study raised questions for you?

D. **Discuss questions selected from the daily readings.**

   1. **KEY OBSERVATION:** Judgment rooted in Christian convictions should yield godly justice.

      DISCUSSION QUESTION: What are some reasons Paul preferred for Christians to do their judging in-house rather than taking matters outside?

   2. **KEY OBSERVATION:** The church is not a shop of secrets, but a house of honesty.

      DISCUSSION QUESTION: What are some positive reasons for having a system of judgment in place within the church?

3. **KEY OBSERVATION:** Allegiance to King Jesus provides freedom in God's presence here and now.

    DISCUSSION QUESTION: What is the significance of believers realizing that they are heirs of God's kingdom in the present *and* the future rather than in the future only?

4. **KEY OBSERVATION:** The resurrection should form the basis of how we think about and treat the body—and not just our own either.

    DISCUSSION QUESTION: Why is treating our bodies and others' bodies in holy ways so important?

5. **KEY OBSERVATION:** The price at which Jesus bought his people was steep.

    DISCUSSION QUESTION: What does it suggest about God that he bought us at a price? What does it suggest about us?

E. **As the study concludes, consider specific ways that this week's Bible lesson invites you to grow and calls you to change.** How do this week's scriptures call us to think differently? How do they challenge us to change in order to align ourselves with God's work in the world? What specific actions should we take to apply the insights of the lesson into our daily lives? What kind of person does our Bible lesson call us to become?

F. **Close session with prayer.** Emphasize God's ongoing work of transformation in our lives in preparation for loving mission and service in the world. Pray for absent class members as well as for persons whom we need to invite to join our study.

WEEK SIX

1 Corinthians 7:1–40

Love and Marriage

INTRODUCTION

In 1 Corinthians 7, Paul continues addressing themes mentioned in chapters 5–6. The major theme is marriage. There are, however, related topics: singleness, celibacy, being a widow or widower, marriage between believers and unbelievers, divorce, remarriage, sex, and lust. He also discusses spiritual gifts, circumcision, uncircumcision, and slavery. Holiness, sanctification, redemption, and salvation are also sprinkled in. There's a lot to ponder in these forty verses.

Additionally, a clearer picture of congregants' identities emerges. Folks spanned the social spectrum. This likely contributed to the division occurring. It is challenging to unite people with different backgrounds, presuppositions, and goals. Nevertheless, Paul believed that unity in the Spirit could transcend these differences and used them advantageously.

Here we get a good feel for Paul's abilities as a writer and orator. He employs a variety of rhetorical devices: comparison, contrast, parallelism, climax, callback, rhetorical questions, greater than/less than logic, and hypothetical reasoning. He puts *logos* (logical appeal) and *pathos* (emotional appeal) to work as he speaks confidently and firmly about the Christian *ethos* (ethical appeal) desired for the Corinthian congregation. He does all that within the span of forty verses! So, as you prepare to tune in, as they say at the movies, "Enjoy the show!"

ONE

Come Together

1 Corinthians 7:1–7 NIRV *Now I want to deal with the things you wrote me about. Some of you say, "It is good for a man not to have sex with a woman." ²But since there is so much sexual sin, each man should have his own wife. And each woman should have her own husband. ³A husband should satisfy his wife's sexual needs. And a wife should satisfy her husband's sexual needs. ⁴The wife's body does not belong only to her. It also belongs to her husband. In the same way, the husband's body does not belong only to him. It also belongs to his wife. ⁵You shouldn't stop giving yourselves to each other except when you both agree to do so. And that should be only to give yourselves time to pray for a while. Then you should come together again. In that way, Satan will not tempt you when you can't control yourselves. ⁶I say those things to you as my advice, not as a command. ⁷I wish all of you were like me. But you each have your own gift from God. One has this gift. Another has that.*

Key Observation. Christians must exercise self-control.

Understanding the Word. The overarching point of chapter 7 is found in verses 32–35. Paul says that by being single, like him, one can live in undivided devotion to the Lord. Marriage, sex, and relationships can distract one from living for the Lord in a single-minded way.

In 7:1–7 there are several prominent issues. First, Paul was not against marriage and sex. He was against sex *outside of* marriage and sexual activity not between a married man and woman.

Second, marriage is a relationship based on sacrifice. In Paul's world men often dominated. Women were often treated as second- or third-class citizens. Some viewed wives as the property of their husbands. Paul offers an alternative view. Within marriage, the husband and the wife are on the same level, even regarding sex.

Third, Paul had a high view of self-control. There were discussions among religious folks in antiquity about how many times a week a couple should have sex. Paul gives no specific number; instead, he says if one partner had sexual desires while the other sought a time of extended prayer, the latter should be respected. That individual should exercise self-control. In fact, both parties should pray. This would help prevent giving in to possible temptations. (Most likely, Paul uses prayer as a general example. Any spiritual act calling for a time of focused attention probably applies.)

Fourth, the statement "I say this as a concession, not a command" is important. This shows that Paul is aware of when he was offering a command versus a concession.

Fifth, Paul's comment that he wished more were like him was characteristic (e.g., 4:16; 7:8; 11:1). This suggested that Paul was single, celibate, and able to live for the Lord in an undivided way.

Sixth, Paul speaks of each person as having a gift. The word is *charism*. It appears in various places throughout both Corinthian epistles. For Paul, speaking in foreign languages was a *charism* (1 Cor. 12:8–10) sometimes linked to prayer/praying (14:13ff). Paul is not saying that marriage and/or celibacy are a person's spiritual gifts (i.e., *charisms*). He is referring to prayer, especially as it is related to speaking in foreign tongues.

Never does Paul refer to marriage or celibacy as a gift. Thinking along these lines would likely lead one to the conclusion that being a virgin, a widow, or a divorced person, or being married to a non-believing spouse is a *charism*. Nope!

Here we must combine some facts: (1) Paul prayed in foreign languages; (2) he was a celibate; and (3) he repeatedly called for his hearers to imitate him. Some of the married women in the congregation who were imitating Paul were abstaining from sex with their spouse. In the letter sent to Paul, they directed this matter specifically to him. They had even created their own slogan. Paul wrote, providing instructions on how to navigate this issue. Later, he tells the married couples that they are to stay together. They should not divorce. Further, they should not deprive one another, not even to be like Paul.

1. What are some of the strengths of either being single or married and living for the Lord?
2. How do the issues surrounding baptism, which were noted at the start of the letter, continue to create problems such as those mentioned in these verses?

TWO

Let It Be

1 Corinthians 7:8–17 NIRV *I speak now to those who are not married. I also speak to widows. It is good for you to stay single like me. ⁹But if you can't control yourselves, you should get married. It is better to get married than to burn with desire.*

¹⁰I give a command to those who are married. It is a direct command from the Lord, not from me. A wife must not leave her husband. ¹¹But if she does, she must not get married again. Or she can go back to her husband. And a husband must not divorce his wife.

¹²I also have something to say to everyone else. It is from me, not a direct command from the Lord. Suppose a brother has a wife who is not a believer. If she is willing to live with him, he must not divorce her. ¹³And suppose a woman has a husband who is not a believer. If he is willing to live with her, she must not divorce him. ¹⁴The unbelieving husband has been made holy through his wife. The unbelieving wife has been made holy through her believing husband. If that were not the case, your children would not be pure and "clean." But as it is, they are holy.

¹⁵But if the unbeliever leaves, let that person go. In that case, the believer does not have to stay married. God wants us to live in peace. ¹⁶Wife, how do you know if you can save your husband? Husband, how do you know if you can save your wife?

¹⁷But each believer should live in whatever situation the Lord has given them. Stay as you were when God chose you. That's the rule all the churches must follow.

Key Observation. Marriage, like singleness, is a means of glorifying God.

Understanding the Word. In Western society, the concept of marriage is changing dramatically. It looks nothing like it has for the bulk of history. Same-sex marriage has been pushed front and center. Its proponents have aggressively tried to redefine the institution of marriage. Following close behind are advocates of polygamy (related to polyamory and plural marriage), incest, and even those wishing to marry non-human and inanimate objects.

Some argue that marriage should not exist. Their agenda is to destroy traditional marriage.

First Corinthians 7:8–17 is concerned with marriage among God's people. The Corinthian congregants had asked Paul about such issues. He viewed marriage as a means of glorifying God. It is also an asset to the church. Paul, after all, was not much concerned with marriage outside the church. Perhaps modern-day Christians would do well to recover a theology in which marriage is recognized by the church alone.

Paul's response was to the church only, not everyone. The theology is Christian as are the ethics. This is not a situation ethics course for non-believers. The apostle responds to several groups. His first response is to widows and/or the unmarried. In his view, they were better off staying as they were. They did no wrong, however, if they chose to (re)marry a believer. His second response is to those already married but possibly separated (not divorced). During the separation, a spouse must not marry another. Reconciling with their spouse is the option given.

This raises questions about circumstances permitting a believer to separate, divorce, and perhaps remarry. Paul's reference to the Lord's command is a reference to Jesus's teachings (preserved in Matt. 5 and Mark 10). Jesus's teaching about divorce certificates prevented men from taking advantage of women during divorce. A valid certificate prevented one spouse from taking everything and leaving the other homeless, penniless, and starving. There were valid and invalid reasons for divorcing. Appointed church judges helped decide such matters.

His third response is to those who were now believers but previously (re)married an unbelieving spouse. While Paul did not sanction believers marrying non-believers after becoming a Christian (1 Cor. 6:15 and 7:39), such a marriage is still valid. The two should not divorce. Why? Because the believing spouse is "sanctifying" the unbelieving spouse—language possibly borrowed from Jewish wedding ceremonies.

Sanctification concerns one's movement toward God. In a marriage of two unbelievers, neither spouse is moving toward God but away. In a marriage with one believer, that spouse can cultivate an atmosphere for the non-believing spouse to encounter God. The same is true of children in such a home. The unbelieving spouse sees God lived out in their spouse's life. This may eventually lead them to choose salvation in Christ. This is akin to prevenient or preventive grace—grace that draws persons to God prior to their acceptance or acknowledgment of him.

Paul says each believer should remain as they are. This is the rule of thumb in every congregation. Again, Paul is focusing on churches, not the rest of society. His imperatives are for believers, not those outside the Christian movement. Of course, evangelizing outsiders and helping them see their sinful ways was still necessary. But discipling disciples is different than trying to discipline non-believers. That is as true now as when Paul wrote these verses.

1. What does it look like to value marriage as a God-ordained institution within the church?
2. How does one successfully balance sharing the gospel with outsiders with not judging them by Christian standards?

THREE
Situation Ethics?

1 Corinthians 7:18–26 *Was a man already circumcised when he was called? He should not become uncircumcised. Was a man uncircumcised when he was called? He should not be circumcised. ^{19}Circumcision is nothing and uncircumcision is nothing. Keeping God's commands is what counts. ^{20}Each person should remain in the situation they were in when God called them.*

^{21}Were you a slave when you were called? Don't let it trouble you—although if you can gain your freedom, do so. ^{22}For the one who was a slave when called to faith in the Lord is the Lord's freed person; similarly, the one who was free when called is Christ's slave. ^{23}You were bought at a price; do not become slaves of human beings. ^{24}Brothers and sisters, each person, as responsible to God, should remain in the situation they were in when God called them.

^{25}Now about virgins: I have no command from the Lord, but I give a judgment as one who by the Lord's mercy is trustworthy. ^{26}Because of the present crisis, I think that it is good for a man to remain as he is.

Key Observation. Contentment in every situation pleases God.

Understanding the Word. The final words of the scripture highlight Paul's cadence. Speaking to various groups, he ends each admonishment with a similar statement: "Remain." He intertwines "remaining" with the notion of being "called by God." That "call" (1 Cor. 1:2), for every believer, is sanctification and holiness. It remains the same today!

Many congregants in Corinth had different vocations. These didn't necessarily change when they became believers. Their social status, however, could have. Thus, he urged them, in whatever circumstances they found themselves, to proceed in their calling. Sanctification and holiness should infiltrate and saturate their lives.

The apostle was not speaking about being a passive Christian. He encouraged contentment in every situation. Circumcision and uncircumcision were not paths to holiness. Nor were they means of "getting in" on the new covenant. Contrary to what some religious officials were teaching, Paul claims that no reason existed for the uncircumcised to become circumcised. It is not these acts that God desires but sanctification. The same thing goes for being a virgin (or not). God desires holiness in state.

Paul addresses slaves here too. This tells us that there were slaves within the congregation. Paul's repeated references to "the weak" throughout this letter (1 Cor. 1:25, 27; 4:10; 8:7, 9, 10; 9:22; 11:30; 12:22) are references to the slave demographic. These slaves were likely foreigners. As the Roman Empire conquered various lands, they eventually ran out of space within the city of Rome to send foreign captives. As a result, they were sent to Roman Corinth. In Paul's time, the slave population there was sizeable. Recognizing this slave contingency among the church helps us understand various issues that arise throughout the letter.

Despite wrongheaded modern accusations, Paul was against slavery. While he did not lead a loud and angry campaign against Rome to thwart the slave system, here he tells slaves that it is ultimately Christ who bought them. He bought them at a price. He was their master; therefore, believers, if able, should not sell themselves into slavery. Moreover, if they are enslaved and can find a way out, they should. Paul's tactic was subversive in a fly-under-the-radar sort of way. (Note: The advice to slaves to seek freedom is different than his imperatives about marriage, where one *should* remain "bound" [see 7:27, 39].) Paul tells the Christian slaves not to worry about their seemingly low status in society. In the assembly, status does not matter; all are brothers and sisters, and all share the same status in Christ. No distinction should exist between believers because of social status.

Finally, it is worth drawing attention to Paul's "opinions" alongside the Lord's "commands." Paul was being honest as he wrote. As readers, we must trust that his own judgments and opinions, that is, what he identified as not being commands from the Lord, were honest and in line with the gospel. Can something in Scripture merely be an opinion? Well, the apostle made this kind of statement several times (7:6, 7:10, 12, 25, 40; see also 14:37). In context, he himself notes that he gives opinions as one who has the Spirit (7:40). That should settle any discussion over whether to take his advice. Whether we call this "inspired opinion" or not, we still recognize that it is part of Scripture. And, if Scripture is the drumbeat we walk to, if it is the cadence for our lives, then we who also have the Spirit should be in sync with what we read here.

1. How has the call to be sanctified and holy penetrated aspects of your life that you may have never expected it to?
2. What areas of your life are most in need of being infiltrated by sanctifying grace at the moment?

FOUR
A Spouse Divided

1 Corinthians 7:27–35 *Are you pledged to a woman? Do not seek to be released. Are you free from such a commitment? Do not look for a wife.* ^{28}*But if you do marry, you have not sinned; and if a virgin marries, she has not sinned. But those who marry will [have trouble] in this life, and I want to spare you this.*

^{29}*[Well] what I mean, brothers and sisters, is that the time is [reaching its culmination]. From now on those who have wives should live as if [not having trouble];* ^{30}*those who mourn, as if [not mourning]; those who are [rejoicing], as if [not rejoicing]; those who buy something, as if it were not theirs to keep;* ^{31}*those who use the things of the world, as if not engrossed in them. For this world in its present form is passing away.*

³²I would like you to be free from concern. An unmarried man is concerned about the Lord's affairs—how he can please the Lord. ³³But a married man is concerned about the affairs of this world—how he can please his wife—³⁴and his interests are divided. An unmarried woman or virgin is concerned about the Lord's affairs: Her aim is to be devoted to the Lord in both body and spirit. But a married woman is concerned about the affairs of this world—how she can please her husband. ³⁵I am saying this for your own good, not to restrict you, but that you may live in a right way in undivided devotion to the Lord.

Key Observation. The resurrection and ascension of Jesus, along with the sending of the Holy Spirit, have set in motion a new way of living.

Understanding the Word. Have you ever been singing a song only to have someone correct your lyrics? It's happened to me numerous times. I've had many similar experiences with Scripture; I've had to own up to being wrong. That has even happened with the highlighted verses. I had previously read the latter part of 1 Corinthians 7:29 as the NIV offers it: "From now on, those who have wives should live as if they did not." I've fixed that here.

The NIV's rendering misses the mark; it is confusing. If we accept it, Paul contradicts himself. He is not telling those in Corinth that they should live as though they have no spouse. Instead, as the original language suggests, he is clarifying his preceding remark in 7:28. There he says that married persons will face *trouble*. He emphasizes that word. It begins a climactic clause in a triple comparison. It balances out his "as if" comparisons too. The NIV also omits the "and" words Paul used. These form contrasts for mourning, rejoicing, and other words. They are there in the Greek. They should be there in the English too. I have added them.

The "trouble" Paul is referring to in marriage is mentioned in 7:32–35: a spouse may be unable to live in undivided devotion to the Lord. In 7:27–28, Paul references spouses and virgins. He discusses the married first (7:28–35). Virgins are the focus of 7:36–38. First Corinthians 7:1–7 says some were attempting to be so much like Paul that they had abstained from intercourse with their spouse. Like him, they wanted to be "undivided" in their devotion to the Lord. For Paul, seeking this type of undividedness while being married is problematic. It would lead to division/divorce. Paul wanted to prevent that.

This is underscored by his remarks about the time reaching its culmination. What he means by "culmination of time" is that the new covenant had been initiated and change was afoot. The resurrection and ascension of Jesus, along with the sending of the Holy Spirit, had set in motion a new way of living—living that sees the world through the lens of the resurrection. The resurrection reminds us that God cares about bodies and so should we. Likewise, God cares about his creation. Jesus's work exemplified this. Thus, the current form is passing or transitioning, and the culmination has been inaugurated. The final culmination will occur on the great Resurrection Day. Then, all believers' bodies will be changed. This earth will also be finally changed (1 Cor. 15; Rev 21–22).

Those mourning now should live as if not continually mourning. God's kingdom has broken in and the early stages of its culmination are under way. Paul was not saying that the end of the world is close. Nor should we. The resurrection and ascension set the culmination in motion. Jesus can come back whenever. Until then, believers participate in ushering in Jesus's ultimate return.

Thus, whatever one's present circumstances are, they should view them through the lens of the new covenant and its promises (1 Cor. 7:18–26). Whether one is married or a virgin, a widow or a celibate, a life of devotion to the Lord is what is most important. And while marriage can certainly get in the way of this, Paul believed that a married couple could live together in devotion to the Lord.

1. How does a person viewing the world through resurrection-tinted lenses see things differently? Why?

2. According to Paul, the culmination of the great Resurrection Day has already started, and believers are invited to help usher that in by living a life devoted to the Lord. How (or how not) is your life in line with this agenda?

FIVE
Virgin Ground

1 Corinthians 7:36–40 NIRV *Suppose a man thinks he is not acting properly toward the virgin he has promised to marry. Suppose she is getting old, and he feels that he should marry her. He should do as he wants. He is not sinning. They should get married. ³⁷But suppose the man has decided not to marry the virgin. And suppose he has no compelling need to get married and can control himself. If he has made up his mind not to get married, he also does the right thing. ³⁸So then, the man who marries the virgin does the right thing. But the man who doesn't marry her does an even better thing. ³⁹A woman has to stay married to her husband as long as he lives. If he dies, she is free to marry anyone she wants to. But the one she marries must belong to the Lord. ⁴⁰In my opinion, she is happier if she stays single. And I also think that I am led by the Spirit of God in saying that.*

Key Observation. Regardless of one's situation, striving toward single-minded devotion to the Lord is the best.

Understanding the Word. Since 5:1, Paul has dealt with matters related to sex and marriage. He is explicit at times. Reading 1 Corinthians 5:1–7:40 is not for the faint of heart; it takes some boldness. Paul's judgments and imperatives provide a glimpse into the growth of Christian ethics during the beginning stages of the Jesus Movement. For the orthodox, even Paul's inspired opinions reveal how faith was worked out practically. Earliest Christianity, with Paul as a prominent figure, was not into just talking theology. No, belief shaped daily life.

Paul speaks about virgins in 7:27–28 and married couples in 7:28–35. Here, in 7:36–40, he returns to virgins, reiterating that virgins are better off if they do not hunt for a spouse. It is not a sin to marry; singleness is just easier (7:38). But the question must be asked: What does Paul mean by "But the man who doesn't marry her does an even better thing"?

Recall that in 7:28–35 Paul mentions married couples having trouble living with undivided devotion to the Lord. Thus, it is easier for virgins to remain alone. This way they can live in undivided devotion. They will not have the potential distractions of marriage. He is not saying that being a virgin or married is categorically better. His point is: regardless of one's situation, striving toward single-minded devotion to the Lord is the best. A wife and a husband can do this but may struggle.

We also see here Paul's reference to acting honorably toward the person to whom one is engaged. We have already spoken some about the fact that this was an honor-shame culture and that is certainly where this language is coming from. Acting dishonorably toward the soon-to-be spouse that one was pledged or betrothed to could occur in many ways. Perhaps what is in view here is disrespecting the significant other by making inappropriate sexual advances toward them before marriage. Waiting until the appointed time to make sexual advances or engage in sexual activities was a most honorable act.

Paul uses the language of "bound" and "free" to describe married or widowed spouses. The language is reminiscent of slavery. Paul also speaks about remarriage, particularly after the death of a spouse. A widow or widower could remarry without fear of sinning. If someone chooses to remarry, they must do so only with a believer. This teaching is very consistent with everything else Paul says.

Paul says that he made his judgments as one who, like the other believers, has the Spirit of God. He did not merely have an uninformed opinion. He is not arguing from silence. He draws on Jesus's teachings, the Old Testament, personal experiences as a Christian, and plain old logic and reason. Thus, his words could simply be dismissed or shrugged off by those in Corinth. Likewise, those of us reading these words today cannot ignore them. A commitment to orthodox Christianity means holding the apostle's words in high esteem. They are guiding lights for the church. One cannot, in good conscience, reject, twist, or pervert these words and still view oneself as in keeping with historic, apostolic, catholic, orthodox Christianity. After all, the same Spirit that indwelt Paul indwells us. Taking a different view leads to unorthodoxy. It leads to walking in step by and with a different spirit.

1. What are the redeeming qualities of virginity in the life of a believer?
2. How can the church do a better job of celebrating the lives of those who are celibate?

WEEK SIX

GATHERING DISCUSSION OUTLINE

A. **Open session in prayer.** Ask that God would astonish us anew with fresh insight from God's Word and transform us into the disciples that Jesus desires us to become.

B. **View video for this week's readings.**

C. **Ask:** What were key insights or takeaways that you gained from your reading during the week and from watching the video commentary? In particular, how did these help you to grow in your faith and understanding of Scripture this week? What parts of the Bible lesson or study raised questions for you?

D. **Discuss questions selected from the daily readings.**

   1. **KEY OBSERVATION:** Christians must exercise self-control.

      DISCUSSION QUESTION: What are some of the strengths of either being single or married and living for the Lord?

   2. **KEY OBSERVATION:** Marriage, like singleness, is a means of glorifying God.

      DISCUSSION QUESTION: What does it look like to value marriage as a God-ordained institution within the church?

   3. **KEY OBSERVATION:** Contentment in every situation pleases God.

      DISCUSSION QUESTION: What areas of your life are most in need of being infiltrated by sanctifying grace at the moment?

4. **KEY OBSERVATION:** The resurrection and ascension of Jesus, along with the sending of the Holy Spirit, have set in motion a new way of living.

    DISCUSSION QUESTION: How does a person viewing the world through resurrection-tinted lenses see things differently? Why?

5. **KEY OBSERVATION:** Regardless of one's situation, striving toward single-minded devotion to the Lord is the best.

    DISCUSSION QUESTION: How can the church do a better job of celebrating the lives of those who are celibate?

E. **As the study concludes, consider specific ways that this week's Bible lesson invites you to grow and calls you to change.** How do this week's scriptures call us to think differently? How do they challenge us to change in order to align ourselves with God's work in the world? What specific actions should we take to apply the insights of the lesson into our daily lives? What kind of person does our Bible lesson call us to become?

F. **Close session with prayer.** Emphasize God's ongoing work of transformation in our lives in preparation for loving mission and service in the world. Pray for absent class members as well as for persons whom we need to invite to join our study.

WEEK SEVEN

1 Corinthians 8:1–9:27

Paul's Slave-of-Christ Ethic

INTRODUCTION

In 1 Corinthians 5:1—7:40, Paul speaks frequently about sex. In 8:1–11:1, he shifts gears and responds to questions related to food. Paul talks about hunger, thirst, eating, drinking, meals, cups, fruit, milk, bread, meat, and meat sacrificed to idols. It is interesting that, for a group with slogans about the meaninglessness of the body, sex and food are focal points.

The term "meat" is central to this section of the letter. Paul uses two terms for this: *vrōmah* (any type of solid food or the meat from an animal) and *kreas* (dressed or garnished meat). In 1 Corinthians 3:2 Paul contrasts *vrōmah* with *gala*, that is, milk. While some translations use "solid food" (e.g., TNIV, RSV, ESV), others translate it as "meat" (e.g., ASV and KJV). Understanding *vrōmah* as solid food helps us better understand food-related issues.

In 6:13 Paul cites what is typically considered a Corinthian slogan: "Food (or "meat") for the stomach and the stomach for food (or: meat), but God will destroy them both." Paul refers to the group saying this as "the strong." They believed what they ate was irrelevant to their spirituality. The types of meat they consume, namely, high-priced meat often sacrificed to pagan deities, has no spiritual bearing. Paul agrees: "But food [*vrōmah*] does not bring us near to God; we are no worse if we do not eat, and no better if we do" (8:8, author's translation). Yet, he quickly qualifies this: "Therefore, if what I eat [*vrōmah*] causes my brother or sister to fall into sin, I will never eat meat [*kreas*] again, so that I will not cause them to fall" (8:13, author's translation).

In 10:3, Paul uses *vrōmah*, but specifically "spiritual *vrōmah*," likely manna (Ex. 16:31–35). This was true spiritual food because it was given by God. It stood in contrast with regular foods, namely, meats sacrificed to idols and/or pagan deities. These were foods deemed spiritual by humans. When Paul says, "They all ate the same spiritual food," he may be implying that they (i.e., Israelites) as a people shared in this bounty. This stood in contrast to Christian meals in Corinth. His example shows that, when division existed among the Israelites, God was displeased (10:5). The assembly at Corinth was starting to look like them. They needed to shape up and become a body unified by the Spirit (10:6).

These "meat" matters provide us with data about the identities of those in the assembly at Corinth, especially "the weak" and "the strong." The strong were upper-crust locals while the weak were foreign slaves. Some of the latter group, particularly those mentioned in 1 Corinthians 8 who had scruples over meat, may have been workers in the Corinthian *makellōn* (meat market). They may have helped butcher, prepare, cook, and sell meats. Such roles were common for slaves in antiquity. These details will help us see more clearly who the recipients of this letter were and why the problems addressed feature so prominently in the church.

ONE
Table Talk

1 Corinthians 8:1–8 *Now about food sacrificed to idols: [You say] "We all possess knowledge." But knowledge puffs up while love builds up. ²Those who think they know something do not yet know as they ought to know. ³But whoever loves God is known by God.*

⁴So then, about eating food sacrificed to idols: [You say] We know that "An idol is nothing at all in the world" and [you say] "[We know there] is no God but one." ⁵For even if there are so-called gods, whether in heaven or on earth (as indeed there are many "gods" and many "lords"), ⁶yet for us there is but one God, the Father, from whom all things came and for whom we live; and there is but one Lord, Jesus Christ, through whom all things came and through whom we live.

⁷But not everyone possesses this knowledge. Some people are still so accustomed to idols that when they eat sacrificial food they think of it as having been sacrificed to a god, and since their conscience is weak, it is defiled. ⁸But food does not bring us near to God; we are no worse if we do not eat, and no better if we do.

Key Observation. Believers should be aware of how their lifestyles affect others.

Understanding the Word. Paul begins this section by reciting another slogan, which is followed by two more. The first motto of "the strong" asserts that "We all have knowledge." Paul, to the contrary, says, "not everyone possesses this knowledge" (8:7). He is referring specifically to the matter of a lack of knowledge among the weak—slaves working in the meat market. They saw Christian elites buying or partaking of meats devoted to other gods. This caused a crisis of conscience. Paul offers guiding principles for both the weak and the strong.

Several hundred years before Paul (i.e., 300–250 BCE), Timaios of Tauromenium reported that there were around 460,000 slaves in Corinth. Around the same time, Apollodorus wrote *Against Neaera*, which talks about the spouse of a slave cook in Corinth named Hippias. Slave cooks were also mentioned one hundred years later by Plautus. All this was prior to Paul and "Roman Corinth." (Ancient Corinth was destroyed around 145 BCE. It took nearly a century to rebuild. Paul arrived in the early 50s CE. Thus, it was different than when Timaios, Apollodorus, and Plautus wrote.)

Rome's military efforts fueled their massive slave trade. After besieging a city, they captured slaves. Once the city of Rome became overpopulated in the early first century, slaves were shipped to other Roman territories. Corinth became a major outpost for foreign slaves with estimates of about one slave per household. Some slaves worked in meat markets. They were able to provide new delicacies. Such skills may have been prized by shop owners. A foreign butcher/cook was often known as *tettix*. Another term was *mageirōs* (see 1 Sam. 9:23–24 and Lam. 2:20). A *mageirōs* was often responsible for sacrificing animals in the market. Pliny, in his work *Natural Histories* (18.28), mentioned slaves trained as cooks to provide foreign-based meals, which were considered luxuries.

Apollo was the deity of cooks and butchers. His sanctuary at Pyla once had an upper kitchen. There was also an inscription of a *mageirōs* of Apollo there. Outside the sanctuary were statues of butchers and cooks. This aligns with Apollo's title "Prince of Butchers and Cooks" in Aristophanes's work *Frogs* (584). Sacrifices were made to Apollo in Corinth. This was done, presumably, with meat from the *makellum* and fish from the *makellum piscarum* (i.e., fish market).

Many ancient accounts spoke of slaves working in meat markets, even as overseers. Thirteen fragments of cookware and eating utensils from Corinth related to the period of Paul reference a man of slave pedigree (i.e., a freedman) who had a prominent role related to the *makellum*. One type of meat sold in the *makellum* was idol meat. It was sacrificed to pagan deities. Paul calls it *eidōlōthutos*. It was high-quality and expensive. This disturbed the Christian slaves working in the market. The strong were making a social statement by purchasing expensive meat. They were also selfishly consuming it during the Eucharistic meal while the weak were sick and falling asleep (11:30).

Thus, Paul was not primarily focused on Jews and their religious scruples over meat. Instead, foreign slaves working in the meat market knew how the meat was handled for religious purposes. They were concerned that those in the assembly eating this meat were in spiritual danger. They may also take issue with the strong eating and purchasing the most expensive meat to make status statements, especially while some of the weak among them are actually physically weak, sick, and hungry. Paul wanted to solve such problems. If we miss these fine-print details, we miss out on seeing the bigger picture being painted in 1 Corinthians as a whole.

1. Why is it important to show concern to our brothers and sisters in the faith when we see them living in a way that may appear contrary to the gospel?

2. Given that so much of our lives are based around food and sharing meals, why must we make sure our ways and means of consumption are not detrimental to fellow believers?

TWO
The Meat of the Matter

1 Corinthians 8:9–13 NIRV *But be careful how you use your freedom. Be sure it doesn't trip up someone who is weaker than you.* [10]*Suppose you who have that knowledge are eating in a temple of one of those gods. And suppose someone who has a weak sense of what is right and wrong sees you. Won't that person become bold and eat what has been offered to statues of gods?* [11]*If so, then your knowledge destroys that weak brother or sister for whom Christ died.* [12]*When you sin against other believers in that way, you harm their weak sense of what is right* *and wrong. By doing that you sin against Christ.* ¹³*So what should I do if what I eat causes my brother or sister to fall into sin? I will never eat meat again. In that way, I will not cause them to fall.*

Key Observation. Christians should embody a slave-of-Christ ethic: live in such a way that your actions create no opportunities for others to sin.

Understanding the Word. First Corinthians 8:13 functions as the climactic point of this chapter. Everything from 8:9 on builds up to this verse. Let's begin at the end and then look back at 8:9–12. Before that, however, a few more words about Christian slaves in the meat market are necessary. Paul founded the congregation. He was also a leatherworker. He likely met slaves in the market by selling them leather products (e.g., tents, sandals, leather bags for oils, leather containers for spices or tools, etc.). He probably worked in the leather shop along the Lechaion Road, which ran through the city.

During his eighteen-month stay in Corinth, Paul worked with Priscilla and Aquila in such a context (Acts 18:1–3). Perhaps his economic terms (e.g., grace, overseer, redemption, etc.) stemmed from such experiences. The slaves may have sold Paul foods or food wares from the meat market. Some were butchers, cooks, and/or meat sellers. In part 7 of the *Dissertations* of Maximus Tyrius, which predates Paul, the Spartans rejected foreign cooks while wealthy and urbanized Greeks tended to welcome them with delight.

Personal slaves were also hired to be household cooks. Aesop told of a slave cook belonging to Xanthos (*Life of Aesop*). Cato mentioned both a male household slave cook (*On Agriculture* 2.7) and a *vilicus*, a female slave manager who was a slave herself (10.1–11.143). A monument and tomb mention Eurysaces, a former slave who became a famed cook in Rome. The slave Musicus Scurranus had his own slave entourage, two of whom served as cooks. Female slaves worked as cooks, particularly as garnishers (Cicero's *Digest* 33.7–8). Some slaves in Corinth possibly worked as personal cooks, maybe even for the elite in the assembly. It is not unthinkable that they were forced to handle the idol meat and saw the strong eating it.

In 1 Corinthians 3:2, Paul speaks to the strong. He says he gave them milk instead of meat because of their spiritual immaturity. In this context, such a remark would have hit home! Telling them that they were not ready for meat would have left the strong embarrassed and the weak feeling a bit justified. Yet, in 8:9–13, Paul affirms that the strong had the proper knowledge regarding eating idol meat. The problem was their immaturity. That, when mixed with knowledge, created a stumbling block for the weak.

This raises questions about how one person's actions affect others. Paul says that a strong believer should be careful. His/her actions should not cause others to trip, fall into sin (8:9), and have a tainted conscience. The weak considered idols dangerous. While Paul believes idols were really nothing, if a believer's conscience was convicted on a certain matter, they should follow it.

If one of the strong did not violate his own conscience by eating idol meat, did he also violate the conscience of the weak who did not witness it? No. The problem arose when the weak saw it and then engaged in it, thereby violating their own conscience. Paul is not saying the weak could control the actions of the strong. Nor is he saying the strong should operate in secret so the weak do not see them. If such actions were discovered later, this could have compounded the problem.

One should think, instead, in terms of moral judgments and social norms. Moral judgments concern rules that define something as inherently right or wrong. Social norms consist of conventional rules or normative behavior marking the identity of a social group. When such rules and behaviors are violated, it is does not mean it was wrong or sinful. Instead, it simply goes against social principles.

Paul aimed to set up social norms all believers would agree to and live by. All social norms were measured by self-sacrifice as portrayed in the life of Jesus. If the social norm of self-sacrifice is violated, one may well make a faulty moral judgment. If this causes distress that leads someone into sin, then the one who caused the distress has sinned. Sacrificing one's individual freedoms is often the best course of action for others (9:1–27), especially if one's freedom-based acts cause others to violate their own conscience. Thus, intent is important.

Despite spiritual immaturity, the strong have proper knowledge of judging intent. The weak lack it but may eventually come around. In the present, because the strong are capable of judging intent, they should follow the self-sacrificing ethic of Jesus. This is not the same thing as saying, "In a situation of manipulation and abuse, just continue letting a person sin against you." Paul makes it clear that when a person can get out of such situations, they should (7:21–23). In fact, removing oneself from abusive situations is a means of grace to the transgressor. It no longer provides them with the opportunity to sin.

(That is not at all to say that victims create the opportunities for transgressors to sin.) Viewed this way, Paul's slave-of-Christ ethic is consistent: live in such a way that your actions create no opportunities for others to sin. Paul uses 1 Corinthians 9 to reiterate this.

1. What would it look like to adopt the slave-of-Christ ethic as your guiding principle for life?

2. How can sacrificing one's own freedoms often better the body of Christ? When have you experienced this firsthand?

THREE
Patron(izing)

1 Corinthians 9:1–12 CSB *Am I not free? Am I not an apostle? Have I not seen Jesus our Lord? Are you not my work in the Lord? ²If I am not an apostle to others, at least I am to you, for you are the seal of my apostleship in the Lord.*

³My defense to those who examine me is this: ⁴Don't we have the right to eat and drink? ⁵Don't we have the right to be accompanied by a Christian wife like the other apostles, the Lord's brothers, and Cephas? ⁶Or do Barnabas and I alone have no right to refrain from working? ⁷Who ever goes to war at his own expense? Who plants a vineyard and does not eat its fruit? Or who shepherds a flock and does not drink the milk from the flock?

⁸Am I saying this from a human perspective? Doesn't the law also say the same thing? ⁹For it is written in the law of Moses, Do not muzzle an ox while it treads out grain. Is God really concerned with oxen? ¹⁰Or isn't He really saying it for us? Yes, this is written for us, because he who plows ought to plow in hope, and he who threshes should do so in hope of sharing the crop. ¹¹If we have sown spiritual things for you, is it too much if we reap material benefits from you? ¹²If others have this right to receive benefits from you, don't we even more? However, we have not made use of this right; instead, we endure everything so that we will not hinder the gospel of Christ.

Key Observation. Christians must be discerning about the relationships they enter.

Understanding the Word. The political philosophy a country adopts shapes its culture. America's acceptance of capitalism provides the framework for many financial decisions. Marxist or Communist countries function quite differently. In the apostle's world it wasn't communism or capitalism that reigned, but the patronage system. It was based on reciprocity: "I scratch your back; you scratch mine."

This created an atmosphere of competition. Everyday exchanges could become rivalries. In these exchanges, honor could be gained or lost. If one person offered a gift and the recipient failed to reciprocate, they could possibly (but not always) lose honor. A gift-giver could gain honor and claim that the recipient was in debt to him. The patronage system created a never-ending cycle of competitive give and take. In Romans 12:10, Paul puts a positive spin on it saying, "outdo one another in giving honor." The patronage system is the backdrop for 1 Corinthians 9:1–12.

In 9:1–3, Paul makes two points: (1) he is free; and (2) he is the apostle to those in Corinth—something reiterated in the first four chapters. Being free means that, while he is the apostle to them, they have no ownership of him. Within the patronage system, one person was identified as the patron and the other a client. The patron had the upper hand and a higher honor status. Some in Corinth viewed themselves as patrons and Paul as their client. But Paul's slave-of-Christ language did not mean that he was their servant or client. They misunderstand him and his role and rights as an apostle.

In 9:4–6 the apostle asks several rhetorical questions. His point is that, as an apostle, he had personal rights that he was able to use or not. First Corinthians 9:6 reinforces this: "Or is it only I and Barnabas who lack the right to not work for a living?" Paul worked outside of the church to make ends meet. Some in Corinth despised this. They were embarrassed that the man they viewed as their spokesman worked in a lowly tanner's shop. Thus, they offered to provide his income. When he refused, they put pressure on him. Within the patronage system, after all, to refuse a gift could be interpreted as a means of shame. Nevertheless, Paul refused to become the client of the elites in Corinth.

In 9:7–10 he offers a few analogies about working at one's own expense. In 9:11–12 he appeals to the fact that, as the one who planted the church, he could view himself as the patron. As such, he *could* expect a "material harvest" from them. He *could* enforce his right to gain financial support from them. But he refused to do so. Taking their financial support would mean becoming their client. That would hinder the gospel.

What about the support from Philippi (4:10)? In Philippi, there were no strings attached. They did not expect Paul to be their client. Paul was consistent with his slave-of-Christ ethic. Just as he tells the slaves in Corinth not to sell themselves into slavery (7:23), he, too, refused to become a slave-client of anyone other than Christ. To become the slave-client of some of the strong in Corinth would create opportunities to distort the gospel. Paul's principled behavior is in keeping with his point in 8:9–13, namely, that he is willing to sacrifice his own rights for the good of others.

1. How does adopting a slave-of-Christ ethic square with not allowing oneself to be taken advantage of?
2. What is the difference in being a slave of/to Christ and a slave of/to another person?

FOUR
Relinquishing Rights

1 Corinthians 9:13–18 CSB *Don't you know that those who perform the temple services eat the food from the temple, and those who serve at the altar share in the offerings of the altar?* ¹⁴*In the same way, the Lord has commanded that those who preach the gospel should earn their living by the gospel.*

¹⁵*For my part I have used none of these rights, nor have I written these things that they may be applied in my case. For it would be better for me to die than for anyone to deprive me of my boast!* ¹⁶*For if I preach the gospel, I have no reason to boast, because I am compelled to preach—and woe to me if I do not preach the gospel!* ¹⁷*For if I do this willingly, I have a reward, but if unwillingly, I am entrusted with a commission.* ¹⁸*What then is my reward? To preach the gospel and offer it free of charge and not make full use of my rights in the gospel.*

Key Observation. Followers of Jesus should relinquish social rights that contradict the Lord's commands.

Understanding the Word. In all of Scripture, these verses are some of the most meaningful to me. When I first became a Christian, 1 Corinthians 9:16 became my life verse. It motivated and shaped me. I remain compelled to preach. Woe to me if I do not! Over the years, I've grown in my understanding of these verses.

The patronage system, for instance, was something I knew nothing about as a young reader of Scripture. I've learned that, within the patronage system, every worker had a right to be compensated for their labors. Paul refers to this in 1 Timothy 5:18. He says that a worker is worthy of his wage. Jesus's words are similar in Matthew 10:10 and Luke 10:7. This is noteworthy because Paul's comments about the Lord's command in 1 Corinthians 9:14 came directly from Jesus. Jesus instructed his disciples on how to conduct ministry in his name. This formed the bedrock of Paul's thoughts on ministry.

With that in mind, there are two things this section of 1 Corinthians 9 is not: namely, a digression or an instance of Paul disobeying the Lord. Here, Paul reiterates the slave-of-Christ ethic mentioned in 8:8–13. The apostle distinguishes between a divine command and an earthly right. Paul's patron was Christ. He was Christ's client only. As such, he would obey the Lord's commands.

Thus, when Paul had a societal right that conflicted with a command from the Lord (e.g., Matt. 10:8), his thought was: "Woe to me if I don't do what the Lord commands!" He relinquished his social right in favor of adhering to the Lord's command. Jesus taught, for instance, that preachers of the gospel should be housed by believers as they travel. They should not take worldly possessions along. They should offer the gospel free of charge (Matt. 10:8). This was what Jesus did. This was what he told the Twelve to do. Therefore, this was what Paul sought to do. Paul desired to follow this command to be more like the Lord. Only then could his boast be in and of the Lord. To reiterate: Paul relinquished his social right to obey a social code of a higher order—the Lord's command, which exemplifies the slave-of-Christ ethic.

1. What does it mean for God to be our patron and us be his clients?
2. When have you seen someone relinquish their earthly rights to follow God's commands? How did that affect you?

FIVE
Freely Give

1 Corinthians 9:19–27 CSB *Although I am a free man and not anyone's slave, I have made myself a slave to everyone, in order to win more people. ²⁰To the Jews I became like a Jew, to win Jews; to those under the law, like one under the law—though I myself am not under the law—to win those under the law. ²¹To those who are without that law, like one without the law—though I am not without God's law but under the law of Christ—to win those without the law. ²²To the weak I became weak, in order to win the weak. I have become all things to all people, so that I may by every possible means save some. ²³Now I do all this because of the gospel, so that I may share in the blessings.*

²⁴Don't you know that the runners in a stadium all race, but only one receives the prize? Run in such a way to win the prize. ²⁵Now everyone who competes exercises self-control in everything. They do it to receive a perishable crown, but we an imperishable crown. ²⁶So I do not run like one who runs aimlessly or box like one beating the air. ²⁷Instead, I discipline my body and bring it under strict control, so that after preaching to others, I myself will not be disqualified.

Key Observation. Jesus's followers should not change themselves or their convictions based on who they are around.

Understanding the Word. First Corinthians 9:19–23 is one of the most misunderstood sections of the New Testament. I cringe when people use it as to assert that Paul changed his ministerial practices or altered his beliefs based on who he was with. It is then argued that we should do likewise. That is not what Paul is saying. These comments must be taken with preceding remarks in 9:13–18. Paul bases his ministry practices on the command of the Lord (Matt. 10:8): freely give the gospel.

When someone is preaching, a listener may hear and offer an invitation to stay in their home. Thus, upon entering a town, a traveling preacher like Paul may be a stranger. After hearing Paul, some may welcome him like family into their home. In time, they grow close. Kinship is formed via the Spirit. Their relationship with Paul changes and grows. He becomes a brother in Christ. He becomes someone different to them than he was initially.

That's what Paul means when he speaks about "changing" or "becoming" in 9:20–22. He isn't speaking about changing his ways, views, or practices. He is addressing how the perceptions of him by those whom he met changed. When he says, "To the Jews I became like a Jew" what he means is, "In the eyes of the Jews I met, I eventually ceased to be a stranger. They considered me a family member, a brother in Christ." He also says, "To those under the law I became like one under the law."

He is saying that his relationship with those under the law whom he had met while a stranger changed. Eventually, he was considered kin by them. Likewise, "those not under the law and the weak" eventually considered him kin. In time, some could have taken this a step farther, viewing Paul as a household slave. In 9:19 he says, "Although I am free from all and not anyone's slave, I have made myself a slave to everyone, in order to win more people." Paul had not sold himself into slavery, but freely offered himself as a slave of Christ to others.

In 9:18 he mentions his "reward" as preaching the gospel "free of charge." He did not make full use of his *rights* as a preacher. He says in 9:23, "I do all this because of the gospel, so that I may share in its blessings." As Paul went from city to city, he shared the gospel. Those who heard him trusted him and his message. They came to view him as a family member in the faith. Thus, it was their perspective of him that changed, not his theology, ministerial practices, or ethics.

Change in the ancient world, after all, was typically heavily frowned upon and not easily accepted. Change from vice to virtue or bad to good was often viewed positively but being a turncoat just to please people would have discredited Paul and his message. Such actions, marked by doublespeak and two-facedness, would have been the equivalent of "running aimlessly," "beating the air," and being "disqualified" for the prize (9:26–27). Paul's tack is different. His athletic analogies in 9:24–27 restates what he has been saying since 8:8–13, namely, that his slave-of-Christ ethic is his guiding principle. Those who identify as his kin should recognize, affirm, and emulate that.

1. How is it that being a slave of Christ is actually freeing?
2. What detriment will it be to the gospel if our words and actions do not match up?

WEEK SEVEN

GATHERING DISCUSSION OUTLINE

A. **Open session in prayer.** Ask that God would astonish us anew with fresh insight from God's Word and transform us into the disciples that Jesus desires us to become.

B. **View video for this week's readings.**

C. **Ask:** What were key insights or takeaways that you gained from your reading during the week and from watching the video commentary? In particular, how did these help you to grow in your faith and understanding of Scripture this week? What parts of the Bible lesson or study raised questions for you?

D. **Discuss questions selected from the daily readings.**

   1. **KEY OBSERVATION:** Believers should be aware of how their lifestyles affect others.

      DISCUSSION QUESTION: Given that so much of our lives are based around food and sharing meals, why must we make sure our ways and means of consumption are not detrimental to fellow believers?

   2. **KEY OBSERVATION:** Christians should embody a slave-of-Christ ethic: live in such a way that your actions create no opportunities for others to sin.

      DISCUSSION QUESTION: How can sacrificing one's own freedoms often better the body of Christ? When have you experienced this firsthand?

3. **KEY OBSERVATION:** Christians must be discerning about the relationships they enter.

   DISCUSSION QUESTION: How does adopting a slave-of-Christ ethic square with not allowing oneself to be taken advantage of?

4. **KEY OBSERVATION:** Followers of Jesus should relinquish social rights that contradict the Lord's commands.

   DISCUSSION QUESTION: When have you seen someone relinquish their earthly rights to follow God's commands? How did that affect you?

5. **KEY OBSERVATION:** Jesus's followers should not change themselves or their convictions based on who they are around.

   DISCUSSION QUESTION: What detriment will it be to the gospel if our words and actions do not match up?

E. **As the study concludes, consider specific ways that this week's Bible lesson invites you to grow and calls you to change.** How do this week's scriptures call us to think differently? How do they challenge us to change in order to align ourselves with God's work in the world? What specific actions should we take to apply the insights of the lesson into our daily lives? What kind of person does our Bible lesson call us to become?

F. **Close session with prayer.** Emphasize God's ongoing work of transformation in our lives in preparation for loving mission and service in the world. Pray for absent class members as well as for persons whom we need to invite to join our study.

WEEK EIGHT

1 Corinthians 10:1–11:1

More on Food and Idols

INTRODUCTION

On his 1968 album titled "The Holy Land," the legendary Johnny Cash recorded a song titled "Daddy Sang Bass." It became an immediate hit. In 1 Corinthians 10, Paul often sings in harmony with Moses. Mosaic writings from the Old Testament supply vocabulary for Paul's comments on authentic spirituality, unity, and maintaining fellowship. Moses's works functioned like a movie score that helped those in Corinth see and hear the heart of the conflict among them. While Moses sings bass, Paul sings tenor. The two are in harmony and Paul invites his siblings in Corinth to begin singing along in the same key.

Paul also speaks about orderliness and self-sacrifice. These matters fall within purview of his discussion about idol meat. Some wondered: *If a follower of Jesus does not believe in idols, is it then permissible for that believer to eat food that has been sacrificed to idols (by a non-believer)?* Some viewed Paul's answer as ambiguous and others as contradictory. I believe it is quite clear: Paul forbids those in the assembly from eating food consecrated or dedicated to idols. To substantiate his claims, Paul draws on Israel's history and examples contemporary with his own time. He even appeals to himself as an example. He hopes that those in the know regarding idol meat would lay down their social rights for a higher spiritual good.

ONE
Can I Get a Witness?

1 Corinthians 10:1–6 CEB *Brothers and sisters, I want you to be sure of the fact that our ancestors were all under the cloud and they all went through the sea. ²All were baptized into Moses in the cloud and in the sea. ³All ate the same spiritual food, ⁴and all drank the same spiritual drink. They drank from a spiritual rock that followed them, and the rock was Christ. ⁵However, God was unhappy with most of them, and they were struck down in the wilderness. ⁶These things were examples for us, so we won't crave evil things like they did.*

Key Observation. Christians should take care not to provoke God's jealousy.

Understanding the Word. In close relationships we know how to push others' buttons. We know what stirs their anger and makes their blood boil. We know what hurts deeply. We know how to mock, tease, and taunt. We know how to get their attention to invoke jealousy. When we're not in close relationships, discerning these things is more difficult.

Paul talks about idol meat in 1 Corinthians 10 just as he does two chapters earlier. Here he speaks about why idol meat should not be eaten by believers. He says that partaking of such foods may provoke God's jealousy. He wonders why anyone would take such a risk; it is simply too dangerous. Why chance pushing God's buttons and/or devastating one's relationship with him?

Paul draws on Israel's past to make his point. He says the Israelites underwent one baptism. It was a baptism with Moses in which all partook of the same spiritual gifts. This is a reference to the Exodus event (13–14). In 1 Corinthians 1:10–31, Paul connects baptism to spiritual gifts, which were at the center congregational dissension. Whereas the Israelites had one baptism and partook of the same spiritual gifts, those in Corinth were fighting about baptisms and gifts. By focusing on the gifts and what honor they brought, God, the gift giver, was overlooked. This provoked his righteous jealousy.

Similarly, issues with idol meat had arisen. The so-called spiritually mature claimed to know there's no problem consuming these. The weak, that is, the foreign slaves, were troubled by this. Paul agrees with the strong that there are no idols. Yet, he ultimately sides with the weak. The knowledge that Paul identifies as a spiritual gift (1 Cor. 1:5) has been abused in two ways: (1) it has prevented the strong from considering the best interests of others first, and (2) it has brought focus to the gift and the one having it rather than God, the giver.

These are grounds for provoking God's jealousy. Why chance it? Those in Corinth should consider what happened among the Israelites. Given their behavior, worse things may befall them. Those events are types of what it looks like when God's jealousy is provoked (see also 10:11). By learning from them, those in Corinth could spare themselves heartache and hardship. The Israelites, too, are "types" (or archetypes) of those in Corinth. Moreover, the rocks that Israel drew water from at Rephidim (Ex. 17) and Kadesh (Num. 20:11) are both "types" of Jesuses. Paul is not saying that Jesus was traveling with the Israelites as a rolling rock (although, the "cloud" here could allude to the Spirit voyaging with them in cloud form).

Paul is suggesting that, if the Corinthians allow these stories to speak to their present circumstances, they would both be putting themselves in the Israelite's sandals and remaining in the present. It is like reuniting with a friend thirty years later. They come back into our lives and remind us of our past stories. They talk about how we look and act the same yet different. They bring the past immediately into the present. The person we were before was but a shadow, a type of who we are now. Israel and the rock were earlier types of the church and the Anointed One. It was the Rock, not the Israelites, that those in Corinth needed as a model.

1. What does it suggest about the nature and character of God that he is jealous?
2. Can jealousy ever be a healthy thing? If so, how? If not, why?

TWO
The Temptations

1 Corinthians 10:7–15 *Do not be idolaters, as some of them were; as it is written: "The people sat down to eat and drink and got up to indulge in revelry." ⁸We should not commit sexual immorality, as some of them did—and in one day twenty-three thousand of them died. ⁹We should not test Christ, as some of them* did—and were killed by snakes. ¹⁰And do not grumble, as some of them did—and were killed by the destroying angel.

¹¹These things [were typological occurrences] and were written down as warnings for us, on whom the culmination of the ages has come. ¹²So, if you think you are standing firm, be careful that you don't fall! ¹³No temptation has overtaken you except what is [man-made]. And God is faithful; he will not let you [all] be tempted beyond what you [are able to endure, but with the temptation he will even make a way out to be able to endure.]

¹⁴Therefore, my dear friends, flee from idolatry. ¹⁵I speak to sensible people; judge for yourselves what I say.

Key Observation. Spiritual gifts should be used to sustain and unite one another rather than to divide.

Understanding the Word. Recently, a business trend has emerged in America. The premise? Customers pay hundreds of dollars to be locked in a room for an hour and, if they can figure out how to escape, they win. Actually, they don't win anything beyond bragging rights. I suppose I could be forgiven for doubting that this business would succeed but, alas, thus far it has. Here Paul speaks of something similar, namely, escaping. He speaks about escaping a temptation-laden situation. First Corinthians 10:13 is quoted often but quite misunderstood. While God may provide ways to deliver us from temptation, that is not what this verse claims.

We must bear in mind the overarching point: 1 Corinthians 8:1–11:1 is, in general, about eating idol meat. Likewise, 10:13 in particular, is also about eating idol meat. First Corinthians 10:14 proves this: "Therefore, my dear friends, flee from idolatry." There is also a clue in 10:13, which is often missed because English translations fail to capture it and many only cite the latter half of the verse. It is the word *man-made*. Paul says all temptations are man-made. Idols are man-made entities. Meat sacrificed to idols has become a temptation to some in Corinth.

These are man-made temptations, not God-made. God, in his goodness, kindness, and love, provides believers a way to escape from these temptations. In the same way he provided a way out for the Israelites, he will provide a way out for the Corinthians. The way out is giving up one's social rights for a higher cause. And, although God has provided a way out, believers must accept that gift and choose to put it to use. God initiates the way out, but believers must choose whether to act. The way out is a means of escape from temptation. One can either choose to walk in a realm where privileging oneself is an inherent trait, or in a realm where self-sacrifice is an inherent trait. Jesus walked in the latter, as did Paul.

Other traits inherent to the former way are mentioned here, too: sexual immorality, tempting the Lord, and grumbling against the Lord. The result: some died by engaging in sexual immorality (Num. 25:9), by being attacked by snakes (Num. 21:5–6), and by way of the destroying angel (Ex. 12:23). These events stood as typological examples. They functioned as warnings for the faithful in Corinth. Yet, just as God provided the Israelites a way out via the exodus event, he offers believers facing idolatry a way out too. It comes by way of sacrificing one's life to God through baptism and receiving both the gift of the Holy Spirit and spiritual gifts. These gifts should be used to sustain and unite one another rather than to divide. These gifts should also be used to assist in overcoming any man-made temptations brought about by idols or idol meat.

1. What is significant about the fact that all temptations, such as idolatry, are man-made rather than God-made?
2. Why is it important that the church be marked and recognized by sacrificing their social rights and privileges for one another (for a higher cause)?

THREE
Bread Ties

1 Corinthians 10:16–22a *Is not the cup of thanksgiving for which we give thanks a participation in the blood of Christ? And is not the bread that we break a participation in the body of Christ?* [17]*Because there is one loaf, we, who are many, are one body, for we all share the one loaf.*
[18]*[Look at Israel according to the flesh: Are not those eating the sacrifices participants] in the altar?* [19]*Do I mean then that food sacrificed to an idol is anything, or that an idol is anything?* [20]*No, but the sacrifices of pagans are offered*

to demons, not to God, and I do not want you to be participants with demons. ²¹You cannot drink the cup of the Lord and the cup of demons too; you cannot have a part in both the Lord's table and the table of demons. ²²ᵃAre we trying to arouse the Lord's jealousy?

Key Observation. No person or entity is permitted to encroach upon one's allegiance to God.

Understanding the Word. Meals bring people together. Imagine dates, holidays, weddings, banquets, and get-togethers without food. Meals provide opportunities to share with others. If someone pays for your meal, especially if it's unexpected, it can be quite meaningful. Inviting someone to a meal is also inviting them to participate in our lives. Around meal tables we pray, laugh, talk, and share. It was the same in antiquity. When the earliest Christians had meals together, they were meaningful. It was then that they participated in the feast of the Lord's Supper. For the earliest Christians, Communion took place around the meal table.

In 1 Corinthians 10:16–22, a section still focused on idol meat, Paul alludes to Communion. He repeatedly uses words related to participation. Drinking the cup and eating the bread are acts of participation in the body and blood of Christ. He does not mean that the bread and/or juice literally contain the Lord. If we follow his logic, in fact, one could conclude that such a view would have been (borderline) idolatrous.

Man-made things have the potential to be idolatrous (e.g., Deut. 4:28; Ps. 115; and Isa. 44:12–20). Idols are nothing more than their essence: wood, juice, bread, or stone. Yet, just as one can devote bread and juice to the Lord, one can also dedicate things like wood, stone, or meat to demons. These demons, in Paul's view, were associated with other spirits. Paul did not believe that other deities truly exist. He did believe, however, that other spirits exist. And when one participates in a meal dedicated to these spirits, they risk committing idolatry. They also run the risk of provoking God to jealousy. Allegiance should be pledged to God alone. No other person or entity is permitted to encroach upon one's allegiance to God.

Instead of being distracted by foods sacrificed to idols, the assemblers in Corinth should turn their focus to what is most important: "Because there is one loaf, we, who are many, are one body, for we all share the one loaf"

(1 Cor. 10:17). The apostle, waxing poetic here, employs a chiastic construction. A chiasm is a literary device that draws attention to a single idea by placing it in between two repeated ideas. It is like a ham sandwich. The ham is placed in the center between two buns. In 10:17 Paul's literary dish was similar: One Loaf / One Body / One Loaf. "One body" is at the center as the focal point.

Problems arise when the spiritual unity of this "one body" is threatened. Paul orders those in Corinth to abstain from meals that cause such threats (1 Cor. 5:11). Given the fractured situation in the congregation, Paul's emphasis on "one body" is a means of drawing attention to spiritual unity. Believers should not be dividing over meat sacrificed to idols. They should not participate in meals with idols or demons at the center. Some in the assembly, particularly the strong, should spend time focusing on meals together that commemorate their Lord's life. As we shall see, Paul drives this point home in the remaining verses of 1 Corinthians 10.

1. What does it suggest about the nature and character of God that he desires for his people to share meals together and participate in one another's lives?

2. What would a congregation with the mindset of "one body" always as its centerpiece look like?

FOUR
Foods with Benefits

1 Corinthians 10:22b–24 author's translation
We are not his "strong ones" are we?
²³"All food is permissible," you say—but all food is not beneficial. "All food is permissible," you say—but all food is not edifying. ²⁴No one should seek the good of himself, but of the other.

Key Observation. When Christians bring worldly concerns into the church, foist them upon others, and obsess over them, division will ensue.

Understanding the Word. In the last decade, the U.S. has witnessed an economic boom in the fitness industry. Wearable technology, map-marking apps, cross-training facilities, and extreme athletics have created a felt need for people to get and stay in shape. New dieting techniques, food prepping tips, and cooking strategies have also come to the fore. Organizations such as the NFL now promote healthy eating and daily exercise. We must, then, be careful not to project our context onto Paul's. In 1 Corinthians 10:22b–24, he is not addressing such matters. When he claims that not all foods are beneficial, he is not referring to calories but rather spirituality. Paul's concerns over food are not focused on one's physical body, but the body of Christ, the church.

This may require some reading between the lines. In 10:23, for instance, Paul says, "'All food is permissible for me,' you say—but all food is not beneficial to the other. 'All food is permissible for me,' you say—but all food is not edifying to the other." This is reinforced in 10:24, "No one should seek the good of himself, but of the other." Key here is the contrast between "me" and "the other."

As Paul talks about idol meat, he tells those in Corinth, particularly the strong, that they need to adopt the guiding principle of putting "the other" before themselves. He has, in a way, been saying this all along. He reiterates his earlier point: relinquishing social privileges for the sake of a sibling in Christ is rooted in the slave-of-Christ ethic. When social privileges run contrary to the gospel, those social privileges should be relinquished. Gospel ethics always trump social privileges.

One of the mottos of the strong was "All food is permissible." Buying and eating expensive food was a social privilege. Doing so while knowing that a brother or sister in Christ was hungry could be a form of injustice. It could be even more unjust if that sibling was the one selling the food. The meal may be beneficial to the one buying it, but not the one selling it. Paul would rather see believers sharing meals together. Thus, relinquishing a social privilege for the cause of Christ was what's most important.

Buying and/or eating food sacrificed to idols may be socially permissible. It may also be a gateway into dining at the table of demons, thereby provoking God's jealousy. That, in no way, edifies the church. As such, every believer should be willing to let go of this social right and adhere to the slave-of-Christ ethic for the greater good. This was Paul's own practice. He wanted everyone in Corinth to adopt it (11:1).

Followers of Jesus must be willing to put the gospel above any social advantage. It is not the Christian's agenda to contend for social privileges.

Nor is it the Christian's agenda to concern themselves with what the world considers advantageous. The Christian's cause is the gospel and unity in the church via the Spirit. When Christians bring worldly concerns into the church, foist them upon others, and obsess over them, division will ensue. In Corinth, an emphasis inside the church on outside social privileges, such as consuming idol meat, became divisive. Today, the church often gets itself caught up in distracting social and political issues too. Christians need not focus on how the world operates, but how the body of Christ operates. Matters outside the church tend to be distractions that prevent the body from being healthy and fit.

1. When a social privilege or right conflicts with the gospel what should the Christian's immediate and innate reaction be? Why?
2. How can you look after your brothers and sisters in Christ today?

FIVE
Conscientious Objectors

1 Corinthians 10:25–11:1 *Eat anything sold in the meat market without raising questions of conscience, ²⁶for, "The earth is the Lord's, and everything in it."*

²⁷If an unbeliever invites you to a meal and you want to go, eat whatever is put before you without raising questions of conscience. ²⁸But if someone says to you, "This [is an idol] sacrifice," then do not eat it, both for the sake of the one who told you and for the sake of conscience. ²⁹I am referring to the other person's conscience, not yours. For [what reason is my social freedom] being judged by another's conscience? ³⁰If I take part in the meal with thankfulness, why am I [blasphemed] because of something I thank God for?

³¹So whether you eat or drink or whatever you do, do it all for the glory of God. ³²Do not cause anyone to stumble, whether Jews, Greeks or the church of God—³³even as I try to please everyone in every way. For I am not seeking my own good but the good of many, so that they may be [preserved.] ¹¹:¹Follow my example, as I follow the example of Christ.

Key Observation. Christians must not make an idol of a clean conscience.

Understanding the Word. As a pastor, invitations to meals can be exciting and terrifying. They can be terrifying because you never know what someone might put in their meatloaf. During one home visit, a woman offered me outdated milk and stale cake. I tried to down the food, but I just could not eat it all. When I later shared this with an elder, he partially cited 1 Corinthians 10:27 in question form: "Doesn't Scripture say, 'eat whatever is put before you?'" His was not in jest; he was serious. He feared that, as a representative of the congregation, I would become an embarrassment by rejecting meals. He wanted me to eat whatever came my way. A close reading, however, reveals that Paul's point is quite different.

First, the apostle is still discussing meat sacrificed to idols. (Stale cake and outdated milk are not comparable.) Second, Paul's comment has to do with conscience, that is, a moral decision concerning the consumption of idol meat. Third, eating with unbelievers, not believers, was in view. And fourth, the overall point is: if my dining/social privileges are detrimental to a sibling in the faith, I should relinquish them. Why? Because I could potentially damage someone else's conscience by my actions. Christians should always be ready to forego their social privileges for the sake of a brother or sister in Christ.

Paul uses the word "conscience" several times. It is the same word used in 1 Corinthians 8:7–12. He is speaking mainly to the strong in the congregation. In principle, he agrees that eating meat sacrificed to an idol was not sinful. This is the case because: (1) an idol is nothing; (2) perhaps all meat in the *makellum* was sacrificed to idols; and (3) everything on the earth is God's, including all meat. Thus, if a Christian buys meat, they should go ahead and eat for it belongs to God. Likewise, if they are invited to a meal by an unbeliever, they should go. They may even thank God for such an opportunity.

During the course of a meal, a line was crossed, however, when the point was explicitly made to the believer that the meat had been sacrificed to an idol. Once this happened, believers must abstain from eating. They may arouse God's jealousy, potentially dine with demons, and possibly jeopardize a faith sibling's conscience. Regardless of a clear conscience, it was not themselves they should be chiefly concerned with but offending God and other believers. Concern for God and others informed Paul's statement in 10:31–32: "So whether you eat or drink or whatever you do, do it all for the glory of God. Do not cause anyone to stumble, whether Jews, Greeks or the church of God."

This was elaborated on in 10:33. Paul says that he sought not his own good but the good of many. The "many" here were his brothers and sisters in Christ. He sought their good so that they would be preserved. By "preserved" he means spiritually whole and united via the Spirit. Like Jesus, he put their best interests before his own. He calls for everyone else to do the same in 11:1, "Follow my example, as I follow the example of Christ." The question is: Will you follow this example?

1. What role does the conscience play in the life of the believer?
2. Why did Paul permit Christians to dine with unbelievers who engaged in sin, but not believers who engaged in sin? What does this suggest about the nature of evangelism over and against Christian fellowship?

More on Food and Idols

WEEK EIGHT

GATHERING DISCUSSION OUTLINE

A. **Open session in prayer**. Ask that God would astonish us anew with fresh insight from God's Word and transform us into the disciples that Jesus desires us to become.

B. **View video for this week's readings.**

C. **Ask:** What were key insights or takeaways that you gained from your reading during the week and from watching the video commentary? In particular, how did these help you to grow in your faith and understanding of Scripture this week? What parts of the Bible lesson or study raised questions for you?

D. **Discuss questions selected from the daily readings.**

   1. **KEY OBSERVATION:** Christians should take care not to provoke God's jealousy.

      DISCUSSION QUESTION: What does it suggest about the nature and character of God that he is jealous?

   2. **KEY OBSERVATION:** Spiritual gifts should be used to sustain and unite one another rather than to divide.

      DISCUSSION QUESTION: What is significant about the fact that all temptations, such as idolatry, are man-made rather than God-made?

   3. **KEY OBSERVATION:** No person or entity is permitted to encroach upon one's allegiance to God.

DISCUSSION QUESTION: What would a congregation with the mindset of "one body" always as its centerpiece look like?

4. **KEY OBSERVATION:** When Christians bring worldly concerns into the church, foist them upon others, and obsess over them, division will ensue.

    DISCUSSION QUESTION: When a social privilege or right conflicts with the gospel what should the Christian's immediate and innate reaction be? Why?

5. **KEY OBSERVATION:** Christians must not make an idol of a clean conscience.

    DISCUSSION QUESTION: What role does the conscience play in the life of the believer?

E. **As the study concludes, consider specific ways that this week's Bible lesson invites you to grow and calls you to change.** How do this week's scriptures call us to think differently? How do they challenge us to change in order to align ourselves with God's work in the world? What specific actions should we take to apply the insights of the lesson into our daily lives? What kind of person does our Bible lesson call us to become?

F. **Close session with prayer.** Emphasize God's ongoing work of transformation in our lives in preparation for loving mission and service in the world. Pray for absent class members as well as for persons whom we need to invite to join our study.

WEEK NINE

1 Corinthians 11:2–12:31

Head Coverings, Meals, Spiritual Gifts, and More

INTRODUCTION

First Corinthians 11:2–12:31 is not for the faint of heart. Verses like 1 Corinthians 11:2–17 are problematic for many modern readers. This is chiefly because of cultural and temporal differences. Paul talks about head coverings, perverting the Lord's Supper, and the misuse of spiritual gifts. We must wade patiently through the data and strive to make sense of it within Paul's letter as a whole. To offer somewhat of a spoiler, what we find here has already appeared in the letter: an emphasis on spiritual unity. The specific issues here all come back to that. So, let us not grow weary in encountering this theme again. The church today desperately needs to hear this. Some denominations, for example, are fracturing, and others stand on the precipice of division. Paul reminds us: hold fast to the gospel, sacrifice your privileges for the sake of siblings in the faith, model yourselves after Christ the servant, and rely on the Spirit.

ONE
Over Her Head

1 Corinthians 11:2–16 *I praise you for remembering me in everything and for holding to the traditions just as I passed them on to you. ³But I want you to realize that the head of every [husband] is Christ, and the head of the [wife] is [the husband], and the head of Christ is God. ⁴Every [husband] who prays or prophesies [with hair hanging down from his head] dishonors his head [that* is, Christ]. ⁵But every [wife] who prays or prophesies with her head uncovered dishonors her head [that is, her husband]—it is the same as having her head shaved. ⁶For if a [wife] does not cover her head, she might as well have her hair cut off; but if it is a disgrace for a [wife] to have her hair cut off or her head shaved, then she should cover her head.

⁷A [husband] ought not to cover his head, since he is the image and glory of God; but [a wife] is the glory of [the husband]. ⁸For [the husband] did not come from [the wife], but [the wife] from [husband]; ⁹neither was [the husband] created for [the wife], but [the wife] for [the husband]. ¹⁰It is for this reason [on account of the messengers] that [a wife] ought to have authority over her own head, because of the angels. ¹¹Nevertheless, in the Lord [a wife] is not independent of [a husband], nor is [a husband] independent of [a wife]. ¹²For as [a wife] came from [the husband], so also [a husband] is born of [a wife]. But everything comes from God.

¹³Judge for yourselves: Is it proper for a [wife] to pray to God with her head uncovered? ¹⁴Does not the very nature of things teach you that if a [husband] has long hair, it is a disgrace to him, ¹⁵but that if a [wife] has long hair, it is her glory? For long hair is given to her as a covering. ¹⁶If anyone wants to be contentious about this, we have no other practice—nor do the churches of God.

Key Observation. God is robbed of his due honor when he's not worshipped appropriately.

Understanding the Word. First Corinthians 11:2–16 is, among all of Paul's epistles, one of most perplexing passages. It has been used to silence women in the church, elevate men in the church, ban men from having long hair, prevent women from having short hair, promote sexism, and describe the Scripture as old-fashioned and irrelevant. Some have even suggested that no explanation of these verses is within reach.

In 1 Corinthians 11:2 Paul changes subjects. In 8:1–11:1 he is focused on idol meat. At 11:2, however, he moves to a new topic. To understand this passage, we must first recognize that many English translations are wrong. Thus, I've offered my own. In every place where the NIV used "man" or "woman," I've replaced those with the correct terms, "husband" and "wife." This helps us see that Paul was concerned specifically with spouses.

In 11:10 the NIV's translation "on account of angels" is also wrong. It should read, "It is for this reason, on account of the messengers, that a wife ought to have authority over her own head." The "messengers" here are humans, namely, "messengers" from Chloe's household (1:11) in Corinth who brought questions to Paul in Ephesus. First Corinthians 16:17 identifies these messengers as Fortunatus and Achaius. Stephanus may have been with them. Stephanus and his household were among the first converts in Achaia (1 Cor. 16:15).

To recap: in 1 Corinthians 11:2–16, Paul addresses an issue concerning husbands and wives. This issue, along with other questions, was relayed to him by men who attended the house church in Chloe's home. These men, probably husbands, were Fortunatus, Achaius, and possibly Stephanus. Now, let's backtrack a bit. In 1 Corinthians 7 Paul addressed husbands and wives. Some wives were withholding sexual activity from their husbands. The reason: the wives took Paul's statements to be/become like him literally and, while married, began living a celibate lifestyle. Like Paul, the wives also began praying in foreign languages. They preferred this over sex.

A specific group of wives from Chloe's house church took Paul's injunctions to imitate him very literally. They had even began acting like men/husbands by not covering their heads while praying in tongues (foreign languages) or prophesying. Wanting to be like Paul, they tried to do exactly what he did. (Notice the remarks about baldness and short hair in 11:4–6.) This suggests that Paul was bald or had short hair. Well, these wives began shaving their heads to become like him. This, in fact, is precisely how Paul was described in the ancient work titled *The Acts of Paul and Thecla*!

These actions were alarming to the husbands and likely brought shame/dishonor to them. As a result, problems arose in each home and while meeting in the house church. Thus, the husbands mention it to Paul. Paul offers the wives a corrective. He notes that, in all churches everywhere, the practice of a woman covering her head is followed. He himself does not cover his head, however, because he is not a woman. Similarly, other men should not cover their heads. Because this is part of the tradition handed on to them, however, the women should. The wives glorified God when they covered their heads. Both sexes honor God each in their own way. God is robbed of his due honor when he's not worshipped appropriately. Thus, both sexes were to honor him as only they can. That is true and authentic spirituality.

1. What value is there in confiding in other believers, perhaps even church leaders, when dealing with matters related to Christian faith and practice?

2. How can misunderstanding or misusing a spiritual gift lead to problems within the church?

TWO

Food Fights

1 Corinthians 11:17–27 *In the following directives I have no praise for you, for your meetings do more harm than good. ¹⁸In the first place, I hear that when you come together as a church, there are divisions among you, and to some extent I believe it. ¹⁹No doubt there have to be differences among you to show which of you have God's approval. ²⁰So then, when you come together, it is not the Lord's Supper you eat, ²¹for when you are eating, some of you go ahead with your own private suppers. As a result, one person remains hungry and another gets drunk. ²²Don't you have homes to eat and drink in? Or do you despise the church of God by humiliating those who have nothing? What shall I say to you? Shall I praise you? Certainly not in this matter!*

²³For I received from the Lord what I also passed on to you: The Lord Jesus, on the night he was betrayed, took bread, ²⁴and when he had given thanks, he broke it and said, "This is my body, which is for you; do this in remembrance of me." ²⁵In the same way, after supper he took the cup, saying, "This cup is the new covenant in my blood; do this, whenever you drink it, in remembrance of me." ²⁶For whenever you eat this bread and drink this cup, you proclaim the Lord's death until he comes.

²⁷So then, whoever eats the bread or drinks the cup of the Lord in an unworthy manner will be guilty of sinning against the body and blood of the Lord.

Key Observation. True spirituality is a gospel-rooted spirituality.

Understanding the Word. Some foods, like syrup and spaghetti, just shouldn't be mixed. The same is true of Coke and Mt. Dew—they don't belong together. Similarly, Christians should not mix what is holy with what is vain.

Such an act is called "blasphemy." Mixing false/inauthentic spirituality with true/authentic spirituality is blasphemy. In 1 Corinthians 12:3 Paul says one cannot mix the statement "Jesus is Lord" with the statement "Jesus is cursed." The end result is blasphemy.

In 1 Corinthians 11:2—14:40, true spirituality is at the fore. The various matters Paul addresses are all sub-categories of this overarching theme. Paul contends that this true spirituality is rooted in traditions and spiritual practices he handed on. In 11:17–27, Paul criticizes mixing practices rooted in vanity with the communion meal, which is sacred and holy. The strong had utilized their elitism to exclude the weak from participating in the communion meal. The strong had even used the excess wine to get drunk. They had made a mockery out of the sanctity of the meal. They had used the holy meal as a means of humiliating their brothers and sisters in Christ (11:22), rather than entering the humiliation of Christ's death. The strong had attempted to mix self-aggrandizement with selflessness. It had resulted in blasphemy (see also 11:28–34).

Paul's comment in 11:17 was somewhat ironic: "Now in offering the following charge, I do not give praise, because your coming together is not for the greater but for the lesser" (author's translation). This was a stinging play on words aimed at the strong. The strong, who viewed themselves as greater, were not coming together for the greater good of the body of Christ. Assembling with the greater good in mind would mean being proactive about including the lesser, that is, the weak. Assembling for the lesser good looked exactly like what was taking place, namely, excluding the weak (the foreign slaves). That's what Paul has in mind when he spoke about communing "in an unworthy manner" and being "guilty of sinning against the body and blood of the Lord" (see 11:27 and 11:29).

There is also irony in 11:18: "I hear that when you come together as a church, there are divisions among you...." "Coming together" stands diametrically opposed to division. One cannot successfully mix unity with disunity. By attempting to do this, the believers in Corinth were defeating themselves. They longed for true spirituality but consistently tripped over themselves.

The apostle reminds them of the remedy by citing the words of Jesus. These words should center them; they should bring them back to the locus of authentic Christianity. Whenever one takes the bread and wine, one is called to remember Jesus. When one's mind is steadied on him, it cannot at the same time be focused on oneself. If one can take that simple principle, which is captured in the Communion event, and let it infiltrate all other areas of life, not only will true spirituality surface but also true spiritual unity. As Paul says in 11:26, that kind of living is a means of proclaiming the Lord's death until he comes again.

1. Based on what Paul teaches here, how might you define true spirituality?
2. Why are self-interest and self-aggrandizement so antithetical to authentic Christian living? What is one practical, selfless act you can do today to help create unity with another brother or sister in Christ?

THREE
A Drink Called Judgment

1 Corinthians 11:28–34 *Everyone ought to examine themselves before they eat of the bread and drink from the cup. ²⁹For those who eat and drink without discerning the body of Christ eat and drink judgment on themselves. ³⁰That is why many among you are weak and sick, and a number of you have fallen asleep. ³¹But if we were more discerning with regard to ourselves, we would not come under such judgment. ³²Nevertheless, when we are judged in this way by the Lord, we are being disciplined so that we will not be finally condemned with the world.*

³³So then, my brothers and sisters, when you gather to eat, you should all eat together. ³⁴Anyone who is hungry should eat something at home, so that when you meet together it may not result in judgment.

And when I come I will give further directions.

Key Observation. Christians' lives must provide concrete examples of what pure religion looks like.

Understanding the Word. Recently, I saw a statistic that made my jaw drop: if every pastor in the U.S. adopted a child in need of family, the world orphan crisis would immediately end. As the father of adopted children, I am, of course, an advocate of adoption. While the nuances of adoption in antiquity were different than today, I still take heart in the fact that looking after those without parents is part of what it means to engage in pure religion (James 1:27).

In a world where some are searching for religion or spirituality while others are striving flee it, Christians' lives must provide concrete examples of what pure religion looks like. Walking in step with the Holy Spirit and living a sanctified life brings credibility to the gospel. It also negates non-Christians' appeals for rejecting the faith based on the claim that Christians are nothing more than hollow, self-serving hypocrites.

How Christians serve, minister, and care for one another is important. Something has gone terribly wrong when Christians fail to care for others, but it is even worse when they shrug off caring for one another. In 1 Corinthians 11:28–34, that's what Paul is talking about. The strong were excluding their siblings in the faith from the communal meal. They had neglected the weak, some of whom were sick and died because of it (11:30). Thus, when Paul commanded each person to examine themselves with regard to the supper, he was not telling them to focus on themselves. He was reminding them to look *past* themselves and *to* their siblings in the faith (11:28–29).

Evidently, some of the strong were hungry and began the meal without the weak. They may have even taken the portion for them. Such selfish activities are, as 11:17–27 suggests, a form of blasphemy. These acts bring judgment upon oneself (11:31). When a person presents themselves in an unholy manner, their actions speak truth about their character. As such, their character is put on display for all to see. Or, stated more simply: they bring judgment upon themselves. Many fail to realize this. It is the Christian's job to help them recognize this, to help them acknowledge the judgment they have brought upon themselves. It is not the Christian's job, however, to pass judgment. That is reserved for God (1 Cor. 5:12–13; 6:2–3; 11:32).

For the Christian, recognizing this judgment is a gift from God. As Paul says in 11:32, "when we are judged in this way by the Lord, we are being disciplined so that we will not be finally condemned with the world." Being disciplined helps us live a holier life now and prepares us for what's ahead. As Jesus's followers, we should look out for our siblings in the faith and foster spiritual unity among God's people.

Paul tells those in Corinth that they would have to wait, until he visited again, to hear the remainder of his thoughts about Communion (11:34). Like most preachers and teachers, Paul likely had much more to say. At the same time, we can be confident that we have not missed out on anything major. Paul's recurring point—living a life of self-sacrifice that is oriented toward serving others and caring for one's brothers and sisters in the faith—comes through loud and clear. Let us respond in a way that exemplifies pure religion, exudes authentic spirituality, and fosters unity in the Holy Spirit.

1. How do a person's actions put their character on display?
2. Describe a time you saw someone looking after another believer. What did that look like?

FOUR
Gift Return

1 Corinthians 12:1–11 *Now about the gifts of the Spirit, brothers and sisters, I do not want you to be [without knowledge]. ²You know that when you were pagans, [you were led] to mute idols. ³Therefore I want you to know that no one who is speaking by the Spirit of God says, "Jesus be cursed," and no one can say, "Jesus is Lord," except by the Holy Spirit.*

⁴There are different kinds of gifts, but the same Spirit distributes them. ⁵There are different kinds of service, but the same Lord. ⁶There are different kinds of working, but in all of them and in everyone it is the same God at work.

⁷Now to each one the manifestation of the Spirit is given for the common good. ⁸To one there is given through the Spirit a message of wisdom, to another a message of knowledge by means of the same Spirit, ⁹to another faith by the same Spirit, to another gifts of healing by that one Spirit, ¹⁰to another miraculous powers, to another prophecy, to another distinguishing between spirits, to another speaking in different kinds of tongues, and to still another the interpretation of tongues. ¹¹All these are the work of one and the same Spirit, and he distributes them to each one, just as he determines.

Key Observation. Jesus's followers should not elevate one spiritual gift over another.

Understanding the Word. The best thing about ministry is the people. The worst thing about ministry can be people. That's part of what makes it so difficult. Everyone comes to Christianity with a different background, personality, and sense of what the church is, does, and should be. It is challenging to leverage all of the differences for one larger cause.

When it comes to 1 Corinthians 12:1–11—a passage a senior pastor once tried to use to get me fired from my associate minister position—I am reminded that ministry is hard. People can be difficult to work with. The pastor was a Cessationist, that is, someone who believes that all spiritual gifts *ceased* to exist when the last apostle died. He put me on trial before the elders and the deacons of the church because I disagreed with him.

He argued that things that appear to be spiritual gifts today are, in fact, deceptions of Satan. He believed that spiritual gifts ceased to exist around the end of the first century. Anything resembling them today, therefore, must represent false spirituality. I was not convinced then and am still not convinced today that spiritual gifts have ceased. Anyone who makes such a claim is, I think, committing a form of blasphemy. Thankfully, the church board agreed.

In 12:1, Paul speaks about true spirituality—a life and practice rooted in the life and work of Jesus and animated by the Holy Spirit. He notes that some in Corinth, who used to live as pagans, now had new life in Christ. They were formerly led to mute idols (12:2). Now they have been led to the Spirit and have encountered a God who speaks (12:3). This Spirit is the one who enabled them to speak Spirit-taught words (2:13). It is only by the Spirit, in fact, that one can utter truth about Jesus's identity as the Messiah.

Folks often ask how they can be sure that they have not committed the unforgiveable sin. My response is twofold: (1) When you sin do you still sense conviction? and (2) Are you still able to confess that Jesus is Lord? If the answer to both is affirmative, that is a good indication that the Spirit is still at work in their lives.

I'm also frequently asked about spiritual gifts. One of the most common questions is: Must one speak in tongues to be saved? The answer is, unequivocally, no! Such a view is a grave misunderstanding of Paul's words. (More on speaking in tongues later.) Nowhere does Paul suggest that speaking in tongues is the litmus test for salvation or true spirituality.

First Corinthians 12:4–6 says, "there are different kinds of gifts . . . different kinds of service . . . different kinds of working." Note that none of them is elevated over the other. In fact, in Paul's Trinitarian thinking, the Spirit, the Lord Jesus, and God the Father are present in these in the same way. Paul used the word "same" three times here and later in 12:7–11. All gifts are for "the common good" (12:7) and God gives to each "just as he determines" (12:11). To elevate one over the other is to totally miss the point of their complementariness and unifying nature.

1. What does it suggest about the nature and character of God that (1) the Holy Spirit gives a variety of gifts to believers and (2) it is only by the Holy Spirit that one can affirm the identify of Jesus as Messiah?
2. Have you ever experienced difficulties in ministry? What was that like and how did you handle the situation?

FIVE

Bodybuilding

1 Corinthians 12:12–31 *Just as a body, though one, has many parts, but all its many parts form one body, so it is with Christ. ¹³For we were all baptized by one Spirit so as to form one body—whether Jews or Gentiles, slave or free—and we were all given the one Spirit to drink. ¹⁴Even so the body is not made up of one part but of many.*

¹⁵Now if the foot should say, "Because I am not a hand, I do not belong to the body," it would not for that reason stop being part of the body. ¹⁶And if the ear should say, "Because I am not an eye, I do not belong to the body," it would not for that reason stop being part of the body. ¹⁷If the whole body were an eye, where would the sense of hearing be? If the whole body were an ear, where would the sense of smell be? ¹⁸But in fact God has placed the parts in the body, every one of them, just as he wanted them to be. ¹⁹If they were all one part, where would the body be? ²⁰As it is, there are many parts, but one body.

²¹The eye cannot say to the hand, "I don't need you!" And the head cannot say to the feet, "I don't need you!" ²²On the contrary, those parts of the body that seem to be weaker are indispensable, ²³and the parts that we think are less honorable we treat with special honor. And the parts that are unpresentable are treated with special modesty, ²⁴while our presentable parts need no special treatment. But God has put the body together, giving greater honor to the parts that lacked it, ²⁵so that there should be no division in the body, but that its parts should have equal concern for each other. ²⁶If one part suffers, every part suffers with it; if one part is honored, every part rejoices with it.

²⁷Now you are the body of Christ, and each one of you is a part of it. ²⁸And God has placed in the church first of all apostles, second prophets, third teachers, then miracles, then gifts of healing, of helping, of guidance, and of different kinds of tongues. ²⁹[All are not apostles (are they)? All are not prophets (are they)? All are not teachers (are they)? All do not work miracles (do they)? ³⁰All do not have gifts of healing (do they)? All do not speak in tongues (do they)? All do not interpret (do they)? ³¹But you are being jealous over greater spiritual gifts even while I am showing you the greatest way.]

Key Observation. If anyone wants to become truly great, they must sacrifice and become a servant of all.

Understanding the Word. Several friends of mine recently started posting weight loss and bodybuilding pictures of themselves on social media. The thing is, these types of posts have a short shelf life. The reality is, the older we get, the more the physique wrinkles up and deteriorates. The desire to show off one's body at a fleeting, temporary moment in time is futile. I think there is more to it. Many want to give the impression that, if they can master and control their body, then they must also have control over their lives. Their body becomes a symbol for a put-together life.

This idea also existed in antiquity. Figures such as Seneca, Cicero, Plato, and Aristotle used the body in various analogies. What Paul says in 1 Corinthians 12:12–31 is, at points, quite close to what Aristotle wrote in his book *Politics*. Talking about the relationship between the city and the individual, he said, "if the whole body is destroyed, the foot and the hand will cease to exist" (1.1253a). The citizens of the city must look out for the greater good of the whole *first* and *secondarily* for themselves. Similarly, with Paul, if one disregards the whole body or even parts of the body, merely focusing on one part, the rest of the body suffers. The good of the whole church must come before the good of a single individual (1 Cor. 12:25).

Building up the body of Christ means acknowledging, honoring, and looking out for the good of each part. Anything less will lead to a breakdown. That, of course, is precisely what's happening in Corinth. There are disputes over spiritual gifts and the statuses they bring. The belief that the gifts received at baptism (and perhaps afterward) were based on who the baptizer was, has caused division and threatened spiritual unity. Here, Paul asks a string of seven questions, each of which expects the answer no! (12:29–30) and then offered a forceful statement: "But you are being jealous over greater spiritual gifts even while I am showing you the greatest way."

They were jealous. They had misunderstood spiritual gifts. The baptizer doesn't give the gift, God does. The gift doesn't signal social status and self-honor; it is meant to honor God. The gifts are not given to create arguments and division, but unity. These gifts should build up the whole body and hold it together. When Paul says they went on arguing while he tried showing them the greatest way, he is referring to exalting God and striving to preserve spiritual unity, even if it meant engaging in self-sacrifice. Self-sacrifice is the greatest way.

The apostle is also addressing the division between the strong and the weak (12:22–24). The weaker parts of the body, those that seem less honorable and easier to dispense with, are indispensable. The strong cannot write off the weak. This is the case regarding Communion, consuming idol meat, spiritual gifts, and the like. Each part of the body is significant. If anyone wants to become truly great, they must sacrifice and, as Jesus once said, "become a servant of all" (Mark 9:35, author's translation). When this is the principle underlying the Christian's every action, the body of Christ will be built up in such a way that everyone will marvel, not at its physique, but rather at its King.

1. When have you been the beneficiary of a brother's or sister's self-sacrifice in the church?

2. How can you become more of a "servant of all" to your siblings in the faith this week?

WEEK NINE

GATHERING DISCUSSION OUTLINE

A. **Open session in prayer.** Ask that God would astonish us anew with fresh insight from God's Word and transform us into the disciples that Jesus desires us to become.

B. **View video for this week's readings.**

C. **Ask:** What were key insights or takeaways that you gained from your reading during the week and from watching the video commentary? In particular, how did these help you to grow in your faith and understanding of Scripture this week? What parts of the Bible lesson or study raised questions for you?

D. **Discuss questions selected from the daily readings.**

   1. **KEY OBSERVATION:** God is robbed of his due honor when he's not worshipped appropriately.

      DISCUSSION QUESTION: How can misunderstanding or misusing a spiritual gift lead to problems within the church?

   2. **KEY OBSERVATION:** True spirituality is a gospel-rooted spirituality.

      DISCUSSION QUESTION: Based on what Paul teaches here, how might you define true spirituality?

   3. **KEY OBSERVATION:** Christians' lives must provide concrete examples of what pure religion looks like.

DISCUSSION QUESTION: Describe a time you saw someone looking after another believer. What did that look like?

4. **KEY OBSERVATION:** Jesus's followers should not elevate one spiritual gift over another.

   DISCUSSION QUESTION: What does it suggest about the nature and character of God that (1) the Holy Spirit gives a variety of gifts to believers and (2) it is only by the Holy Spirit one can affirm the identify of Jesus as Messiah?

5. **KEY OBSERVATION:** If anyone wants to become truly great, they must sacrifice and become a servant of all.

   DISCUSSION QUESTION: How can you become more of a "servant of all" to your siblings in the faith this week?

E. **As the study concludes, consider specific ways that this week's Bible lesson invites you to grow and calls you to change.** How do this week's scriptures call us to think differently? How do they challenge us to change in order to align ourselves with God's work in the world? What specific actions should we take to apply the insights of the lesson into our daily lives? What kind of person does our Bible lesson call us to become?

F. **Close session with prayer.** Emphasize God's ongoing work of transformation in our lives in preparation for loving mission and service in the world. Pray for absent class members as well as for persons whom we need to invite to join our study.

WEEK TEN

1 Corinthians 13:1–14:19

Love and Edification

INTRODUCTION

Recently, a friend posted a link to an article online. The title of the article was "The Most Common Word on Porn Sites Is __." The answer: love. That word has become so overused and watered down that it lacks any sense of depth. The article described how ironic it was that love was the most searched word on pornography sites in 2015. It is ironic because pornography is antithetical to love. Pornography is the debasing of love. It is all about loveless sex. And while Paul does not address matters of sexuality in 1 Corinthians 13–14, he does speak of love.

In 1 Corinthians 13 he writes about love in the context of using one's spiritual gifts. Love, he contends, requires looking out for the interests of another person. Since the basis of using all spiritual gifts is love, believers should use them in the interests of others. He reiterates this in 1 Corinthians 14, where he talks about speaking in tongues, that is, in foreign languages. This gift, like all others, is of a supernatural origin and comes from the Holy Spirit.

Paul himself had received this gift. It is not a so-called "language of angels," but the ability to speak in human languages. (Paul does mention a hypothetical angelic language in 1 Corinthians 13:1, but it is only hypothetical, and nowhere does he say that he speaks it.) For Paul, the gift of speaking in foreign languages is important. He believes that a posture of openness toward this spiritual gift, along with its proper use, is of great benefit to the church. It can help overcome some of the congregation's divisions. It can also help create and foster an atmosphere of spiritual unity. This, of course, is the case with all spiritual gifts.

ONE
What's Love Got to Do with It?

1 Corinthians 13:1–8a *If I [were to speak in the languages of humans and of angels,] but not have love, I am only a resounding gong or a clanging cymbal. ²If I have the gift of prophecy and can fathom all mysteries and all knowledge, and if I have a faith that can move mountains, but do not have love, I am nothing. ³If I give all I possess to the poor and give over my body to hardship that I may boast, but do not have love, I gain nothing.*

⁴Love is patient, love is kind. It does not envy, it does not boast, it is not proud. ⁵It does not dishonor others, it is not self-seeking, it is not easily angered, it keeps no record of wrongs. ⁶Love does not delight in evil but rejoices with the truth. ⁷It always protects, always trusts, always hopes, always perseveres. ⁸ᵃLove never fails.

Key Observation. Spiritual gifts are meant to edify siblings in the faith not oneself.

Understanding the Word. First Corinthians 13:1–8a is poetic and beautiful. It contains familiar lines used at weddings as part of the marriage ceremony. Sadly, however, when these verses are isolated in that way, their original force and meaning are typically lost. We must remember: this passage is a small part of a larger argument. As we know, Paul's overarching point in 1 Corinthians 11:2—14:40 has to do with true spirituality. He exposes vain arguments among congregants about spiritual gifts and status. Thus, while 1 Corinthians 13 is beautiful, it should be viewed as a beautiful rebuke to those quarreling in Corinth. (Not many think of this as a rebuke when they hear it at weddings!)

But why does Paul talk about love here? He is certainly not getting mushy. He wants to make the point that love includes more than one person, it always precludes an other or an*other*. While one can certainly love oneself, that is not relational love. When the congregants debated about whose spiritual gifts were the greatest, relationships were damaged. Relational love was being replaced with self-concern.

The apostle says, if there is no love for one another, spiritual gifts amount to nothing and contribute to the church defeating itself. Spiritual gifts are meant to edify siblings in the faith, not oneself. Abusing spiritual gifts in this manner is the opposite of loving one's brother or sister in Christ. In such a scenario, love has not failed, but one has failed to love. When one puts other believers first, love succeeds. In such a scenario, love never fails.

With this in mind, let's consider Paul's comments in 13:1: "If I speak in the languages of humans and of angels . . ." Paul is speaking hypothetically. The "if" at the beginning of the statement is significant. Likewise, the "and" near the end cannot be overlooked. Because it is a hypothetical situation, we can conclude that Paul did not, in fact, speak in both the languages of humans "and" of angels. The "of angels" part, coming after the "and," shows this is a tag-on. While Paul certainly did speak in the languages of humans, he did *not* speak in the tongues of angels, which is merely a hypothetical example. Yet, even if he did speak both, the result would be the same if he did not speak in love.

The word in the original language is *glossolalia*, which means "speaking different human languages." *Angeloglossy* means "speaking in the language of angels." (Glossolalia is known as polyglossy or multi-linguality today.) Speaking many languages can be acquired through study, immersion, or both. Yet, this can also be acquired miraculously as a gift of the Holy Spirit. It occurred in Acts 2:11, 10:46, and 19:6. This is what Paul speaks of throughout 1 Corinthians 12–14.

Paul, as one born a Roman citizen, would have known Latin enough to converse in it. From his writings, it is obvious that he knew Greek. Likewise, as a Jew, he would have known Hebrew and Aramaic. Some of this would have been acquired through education and immersion in a multilingual environment. Some, however, was given directly and immediately to him as a gift from the Spirit. In dealing with a contingent of foreign slaves in Corinth, such a gift would have been of great help. Even more, using it would have been a means of showing love to the other, the foreigner.

1. Why does love fail, according to Christian thought, when one puts oneself before others?

2. Have you ever seen someone abuse a spiritual gift? What happened?

Week Ten

TWO
Mirror, Mirror

1 Corinthians 13:8b–13 *[Moreover, even if there are prophecies], they will cease; [and if] tongues, they will be stilled; [and if] knowledge, it will pass away. ⁹For we know in part and we prophesy in part, ¹⁰but when [perfection] comes, what is in part disappears. ¹¹When I was a child, I talked like a child, I thought like a child, I reasoned like a child. When I became a man, I put the ways of childhood behind me. ¹²For now we see only a reflection as in a mirror; then we shall see face to face. Now I know in part; then I shall know fully, even as I am fully known.*

¹³And now these three remain: faith, hope and love. But the greatest of these is love.

Key Observation. Spiritual gifts are meant to point to Jesus while we await his return.

Understanding the Word. If we had any doubts before about Paul's beautiful words being a rebuke, 13:8b–13 should resolve them. The apostle's comments about maturing and putting his childish ways behind him (13:11) are directed at troublemakers in Corinth. Paul is not talking about being child*like*. He was talking about being child*ish*. There's a difference. A childlike faith is marked by dependence on God, wonder at God, and a pure love for God. A childish faith is marked by a sense of self-dependence, self-promotion, and selfishness.

The strong exhibited a childish faith. Fighting over spiritual gifts and social status stems from self-interest rather than the interests of the body of Christ. In the city of Corinth, status was important. Stone faces were placed on permanent statues, which lined the streets to signal honor and prestige. When Paul says, "we shall see face to face" (13:12), he was talking about seeing Christ in a similar manner and beholding his honor and glory. In the present, however, we only get glimpses; we only know it in part (13:12).

Paul also speaks of a mirror. This is another example of how important "face" was. A mirror is used to look at and perfect one's face. Of course, mirrors then weren't made with the precision they are now. They only provided, as he suggests, a dim or partial reflection. Glimpses of Christ are partial at best.

Yet, when he returns, all shall see him face-to-face. His return is mentioned in 13:10: "But when perfection comes" refers to Jesus.

In 13:8b–9, Paul mentions prophesying, speaking in foreign languages, and having partial knowledge. Nevertheless, these gifts are meant to point to Jesus while we await his return. These gifts are given to provide others with glimpses of Christ in the interim. No one has the gift or means to fully reveal Christ. People should not act as though they do, for that is spiritually childish. Such actions are rooted in selfishness rather love.

I should say a few words here about Cessationism—the view that all spiritual gifts died out with the apostles. Many Cessationists argue that Paul's comment about "perfection" refers not to Jesus but the Bible. This is incredibly inaccurate and an impossible meaning. Some attempt to argue this from grammar and others from theology. Such arguments, however, cannot stand to reason.

I love and revere Scripture. It is a source of stability in my life. I am deeply committed to it. I submit to its authority. At the same time, I do not make an idol of it. I do not want to commit bibliolatry! I do not worship Scripture; I worship the God of whom Scripture speaks. I worship our Lord and Savior, Jesus Christ. I hold all those views without taking this passage out of context.

Jesus was and is perfect(ion). He lived a sinless life. I worship him. He was perfect in his life, death, resurrection, and ascension, and he will return as perfect. Then I, with all my siblings in the faith, will see him face-to-face, behold his honor, and fall at his feet and worship him. Until then, I have Scripture. It paints a partial but true picture of him. I also have the Spirit, who provides me with spiritual gifts and glimpses of Jesus. For now, then, I long to see him face-to-face. I yearn for that moment when I will know him fully as he already fully knows me.

1. Have you ever experienced rebuke from a Christian brother or sister? Was it warranted? Did it help?

2. When have you seen a childlike faith at work in another person's life? What did it look like?

THREE
Profiting from Prophecy

1 Corinthians 14:1–5 *Follow the way of love and eagerly desire gifts of the Spirit, especially prophecy. ²For [the one speaking in a foreign language] does not speak to people but to God. Indeed, [he is understood by no one, but he speaks mysteries] by the Spirit. ³But the one who prophesies speaks to people for their strengthening, encouraging and comfort. ⁴Anyone who speaks in a [foreign language] edifies themselves, but the one who prophesies edifies the church. ⁵I would like [all of you] to speak in [foreign languages], but I would rather have you prophesy. The one who prophesies is greater than the one who speaks in [foreign languages], unless someone interprets, so that the church may be edified.*

Key Observation. Christians should maintain a posture toward the Spirit that demonstrates their willingness to receive gifts that build up the church.

Understanding the Word. Have you ever heard of "prestige dialects" and "minority dialects"? A prestige dialect is a language or dialect that a community, state, or nation considers the most prestigious. Those who speak a prestige dialect often view other dialects or languages as competitors and treat them with less prestige, that is, as minority dialects. Debates about Spanish and English in certain parts of the U.S. are really about prestige and minority dialects.

Such arguments existed in antiquity too. There were, for instance, debates about whether Greek, Hebrew, or Latin were the most prestigious. The Greeks, of course, viewed their language as the most prestigious. The Romans thought the same about Latin. Greek and Latin speakers held a certain mindset about foreign languages: "If I cease to speak my language in order to speak theirs, I will have moved down the social ladder; I will have lost prestige." A foreigner's mindset, then, was: "If I want to speak or be spoken to, I must learn Greek or Latin."

When foreign slaves were captured and brought to Roman Corinth, they were immediately in a bind. They lacked the ability to speak the local languages. Even more, locals were not going to try to learn their language. In fact, many slave owners refused to help their slaves learn either language because, if they could not talk, they were useless to everyone else and could be kept longer.

We know that slaves existed in the church at Corinth (e.g., 1 Cor. 7:21–22 and 12:13). We know that they were foreign because Greeks and Romans did not enslave their own people. We also know that Paul identified with them (e.g., 9:19, 27; see also 4:1). The foreign slaves, as has been noted already, were the weak. In 1 Corinthians 14, Paul speaks about divisions between the strong and the weak. It's no wonder, then, that the apostle promotes his slave-of-Christ ethic. That would have hit home.

Paul returns to the matter of speaking in tongues, that is, foreign languages. While his words were relevant to the weak and the strong, the latter group was the primary focus. It was not, as is often thought, that those speaking in foreign languages were the spiritual elites. It was the opposite—the foreigners were speaking in their own foreign tongues/languages. But, in 1 Corinthians 14, Paul admonishes the strong to begin speaking in foreign languages. Why? Because they were resisting it. The social elitism of the strong and their desire to maintain their prestige dialect prevented an openness to speaking foreign languages. They neither practiced learning foreign tongues naturally nor maintained a willing posture toward the Spirit to gift them such an ability supernaturally. They were closed off to foreign languages altogether.

In 14:1 Paul exhorts the strong to "Follow the way of love and eagerly desire gifts of the Spirit, especially prophecy." In 14:2 he says, "For anyone who speaks in a [foreign language] does not speak to people but to God. Indeed, no one understands them; they utter mysteries by the Spirit." Those who were open to speaking in a foreign language received two benefits: (1) being heard by God and (2) having the Spirit work in them. Still, the strong resisted this.

In 14:3–4, Paul says that prophesying edifies, comforts, and encourages the assembly. And in 14:4, he says the one who speaks in a foreign language also builds himself up. Verse 5 says, "I would like every one of you to speak in [foreign languages]." The shift from singular (14:1–4) to plural (14:5) suggests that he wanted the strong to be open to speaking more than their own (single) language.

He then he offered a qualified contrast. He said that the person (not the gift!) who prophesies does a greater good than the one who speaks in foreign languages. Why? Because the entire congregation is edified. This qualification is *only* true however, when the one who speaks in a foreign language has no one to interpret what has been said. When an interpreter is present, the one who prophesies and the one who speaks in a foreign language are equal because they both edify the assembly and not themselves.

1. How does lowering oneself in Christian service to others edify them and the body of Christ?
2. Describe a time where you saw someone in the church ignore or relinquish their status to edify the body of Christ.

FOUR
The Sound Barrier

1 Corinthians 14:6–10 *Now, brothers and sisters, if I come to you and speak in [foreign languages], what good will I be to you, unless I bring you some revelation or knowledge or prophecy or word of instruction? ⁷Even in the case of lifeless things that make sounds, such as the pipe or harp, how will anyone know what tune is being played unless there is a distinction in the notes? ⁸Again, if the trumpet does not sound a clear call, who will get ready for battle? ⁹So it is with you. Unless you speak intelligible words with your tongue, how will anyone know what you are saying? You will just be speaking into the air. ¹⁰Undoubtedly there are all sorts of languages in the world, yet none of them is without meaning.*

Key Observation. God expects us to use our gifts to serve him and others.

Understanding the Word. Paul continues writing about prophesying and speaking in foreign languages (one can, presumably, also prophesy in a foreign language!). Outside the assembly, individuals can carry on as usual—in their native tongues. Inside the assembly, however, foreigner speakers need to be accounted for. Linguistic accommodation is needed.

In 1 Corinthians 14:6 Paul puts himself in the shoes of a foreigner. He realizes that, if he were to enter the worship gathering as a foreign slave, he would be rendered useless by the strong. Unless he, as a foreign speaker, had a word of knowledge, prophecy, or instruction for them in Greek or Latin, his presence among them would be pointless. Paul's example aims to get the strong to see things from the perspective of the foreign slaves too. They had been written off by the strong and, as such, were rendered useless in the church.

To bolster his point, the apostle follows up with a few examples. In 14:7, he says all languages have different sounds, just like all instruments do. If people play many instruments at the same time without playing the same notes, the tune will be a mess. Different instruments can work in harmony, but everyone needs to be on the same page. Likewise, within the Christian assembly, speakers of different languages exist. They, too, can work in harmony. For this to happen, however, the language barrier needs to be overcome. Viewing another's language as a minority dialect to maintain one's honor, all the while resisting the ability to speak another's language, only creates noise.

In 14:8, Paul says if the tune of a battle trumpet is not discernable, no one will prepare; no one will recognize it. Similarly, foreigners will not be able to respond adequately to the teachings of the church if all they hear is a language they do not recognize. Those in positions of power or privilege should be willing to linguistically accommodate their foreign brothers and sisters so that they may be edified. Paul was not okay with the strong making a social power play that forces the weak to conform to them.

The points made in both examples are reiterated in 14:9. Paul tells the strong that, if they went on speaking in their own language(s)—probably Greek and Latin—and the foreigners didn't understand it, then they were just wasting their breath. Likewise, the foreigners were wasting their time. Thus, they needed to be addressed in a way they understood. In 14:10, therefore, he says (and I paraphrase), "If you think what I am saying is wrong, just realize that all languages have meaning and are meaningful!" It was not only languages perceived by the elite as prestige dialects that were significant or meaningful. All languages are meaningful. That, at the end of the day, is why the Holy Spirit provides the gift and/or ability to speak in foreign languages.

1. What does it suggest about the nature and character of the church that it should not only be open to speakers of different languages but also open to speaking, either naturally or supernaturally, foreign languages?

2. Why it is important to be open to the Spirit's bestowing of gifts upon us?

FIVE

Tongue Twister

1 Corinthians 14:11–19 *If then I do not grasp the meaning of what someone is saying, I am a [barbarian] to the speaker, and the speaker is a [barbarian] to me. ¹²So it is with you. Since you are eager for gifts of the Spirit, try to excel in those that build up the church.*

¹³For this reason the one who speaks in a [foreign language] should pray that [he may translate]. ¹⁴For if I pray in a [foreign language], my spirit prays, but my mind is unfruitful. ¹⁵So what shall I do? I will pray with my spirit, but I will also pray with my understanding; I will sing with my spirit, but I will also sing with my understanding. ¹⁶Otherwise when you are praising God in the Spirit, how can someone else, who is now put in the position of an [outsider] say, "Amen" to your thanksgiving, since [he does] not know what you are saying? ¹⁷You are giving thanks well enough, but [the other is not] edified.

¹⁸I thank God that I speak in [foreign languages] more than all of you. ¹⁹But in the church I would rather speak five intelligible words to instruct others than ten thousand words in a [foreign language.]

Key Observation. During a worship gathering, all spiritual gifts used must be for the benefit of everyone present.

Understanding the Word. There are many books about the apostle Paul. One has the title *Paul: Apostle of the Heart Set Free*. There is also *Paul: Apostle of God's Glory in Christ* and *Apostle of the Crucified Lord*. One of my own works bears the title *Paul the Change Agent*. If I had to write a book about Paul based on 1 Corinthians, I might title it *Paul: Slave of Christ Ethic and Apostle of the Weak*. As we have seen, much of 1 Corinthians has to do with the weak. Throughout 1 Corinthians, Paul is often on their side. As he continues addressing language matters in 1 Corinthians 14, his affinity for the weak remains. He calls for the strong to put themselves in the shoes of the weak. He wants those in places of privilege to see things from the perspective of those who are not.

In 14:11 Paul says, "If then I do not grasp the meaning of what someone is saying, I am a [barbarian] to the speaker, and the speaker is a [barbarian] to me." In antiquity, the term "barbarian" was an ethnic slur. It was shorthand for identifying speakers of a foreign language. His comment is strategic. Some did not want to lose honor by relinquishing their prestige dialect. Paul recognized that. He says that their refusal to accommodate the weak forces the weak to view them, the elite, as barbarians. In short, they were losing honor. They were losing it in the eyes of the weak. They viewed the strong elite as barbarians, as foreign speakers they could not understand. If anything could motivate an elite Corinthian, it would be fear of losing honor.

In 14:12 Paul echoes 14:1. He exhorts the strong to seek gifts that edify everyone. Self-interest benefitted some but excluded others. Clinging to a prestige dialect in the assembly did not build the entire church up. Yet, Paul did not want the strong to swing the pendulum too far the other way. Gatherings should not be meaningful *only* for foreigners. Paul wanted the strong to allow the Spirit to assist them in speaking in a foreign language. He admonishes them in 14:13 to pray that their speech would be translated. This will be edifying to them and everyone else.

He gives a couple of examples in 14:14–15. The point is: if one of the strong speaks in the language(s) of the foreigners without a translator, it will be fruitless for some. It may be beneficial to the speaker and foreigner, but others will not understand. When someone speaks in a foreign language, it should benefit all the strong. If it does not, then the exercise of the gift is still futile. In the same manner that he did not want the strong to exclude the weak, he also does not want the strong to exclude the strong. He does not want exercising the gift to put anyone, including the strong, in the position of an outsider (14:16). Everyone should be able to say "Amen!" to what a speaker says.

As it stands, the strong were good at giving thanks in their own language. Yet, the other, the foreigner among them, was not edified. The other here is a reference to the weak. In 14:19, he urges the strong to begin accommodating them. In 14:18, he thanks God that he spoke in foreign languages. He did it more than anyone else. He hopes those listening would imitate him in this. He also says, "But in the church I would rather speak five intelligible words to instruct others than ten thousand words in a [foreign language]."

We must fill in some blanks. Here's what he is saying: "In the church I would rather speak five intelligible words to the foreigners, that is, 'the others,' so that they will learn. Five intelligible words can be edifying. If they hear ten thousand words in our language, a language which is foreign to them, they will understand nothing. As a result, they will not receive edification. For that reason, I want to speak to them in their language. But I also want a translator to be present so that everyone else will receive edification, including the strong."

1. What does it suggest about the character of Paul that he defends the weak here and throughout his epistle?
2. Have you ever witnessed an occasion where the use of a spiritual gift ends up excluding people?

WEEK TEN

GATHERING DISCUSSION OUTLINE

A. **Open session in prayer.** Ask that God would astonish us anew with fresh insight from God's Word and transform us into the disciples that Jesus desires us to become.

B. **View video for this week's readings.**

C. **Ask:** What were key insights or takeaways that you gained from your reading during the week and from watching the video commentary? In particular, how did these help you to grow in your faith and understanding of Scripture this week? What parts of the Bible lesson or study raised questions for you?

D. **Discuss questions selected from the daily readings.**

   1. **KEY OBSERVATION:** Spiritual gifts are meant to edify siblings in the faith, not oneself.

      DISCUSSION QUESTION: Have you ever seen someone abuse a spiritual gift? What happened?

   2. **KEY OBSERVATION:** Spiritual gifts are meant to point to Jesus while we await his return.

      DISCUSSION QUESTION: When have you seen a childlike faith at work in another person's life? What did it look like?

3. **KEY OBSERVATION:** Christians should maintain a posture toward the Spirit that demonstrates their willingness to receive gifts that build up the church.

   DISCUSSION QUESTION: How does lowering oneself in Christian service to others edify them and the body of Christ?

4. **KEY OBSERVATION:** God expects us to use our gifts to serve him and others.

   DISCUSSION QUESTION: What does it suggest about the nature and character of the church that it should not only be open to speakers of different languages but also open to speaking, either naturally or supernaturally, foreign languages?

5. **KEY OBSERVATION:** During a worship gathering, all spiritual gifts used must be for the benefit of everyone present.

   DISCUSSION QUESTION: Have you ever witnessed an occasion where the use of a spiritual gift ends up excluding people?

E. **As the study concludes, consider specific ways that this week's Bible lesson invites you to grow and calls you to change.** How do this week's scriptures call us to think differently? How do they challenge us to change in order to align ourselves with God's work in the world? What specific actions should we take to apply the insights of the lesson into our daily lives? What kind of person does our Bible lesson call us to become?

F. **Close session with prayer.** Emphasize God's ongoing work of transformation in our lives in preparation for loving mission and service in the world. Pray for absent class members as well as for persons whom we need to invite to join our study.

WEEK ELEVEN

1 Corinthians 14:20–15:11

The Church: Her People, Her Gifts, and Her Gospel

INTRODUCTION

Paul loved the church. Yet, before his Damascus Road encounter, he persecuted it. He persecuted and possibly killed Christians. He believed he could purify Judaism by exterminating the church. Although that was then, some in Corinth who questioned Paul's status as an apostle reminded him of it. As an apostle, Paul planted churches. After starting the church in Corinth and spending two years there, the church had problems. Part of Paul's solution was to appoint leaders who would render judgments on important matters (1 Corinthians 5–7). In 1 Corinthians 14 he himself offers rules concerning spiritual gifts and their use in worship gatherings. They would create boundaries and maintain order. Paul went from bringing chaos to the church to leading and loving it. May we, too, repent of any harm we've done to the church and, in our turning, love her enough to use our gifts to edify her.

ONE

Are You out of Your Mind?

1 Corinthians 14:20–25 *Brothers and sisters, stop thinking like children. In regard to evil be infants, but in your thinking be adults. ^{21}In the Law it is written:*

> *"[By other-languaged speakers
> and by the lips of others]*

> I will speak to this people,
> > but even then they will not listen to me,
> > > says the Lord."

²²[The foreign languages], then, are a sign, not for believers but for unbelievers; prophecy, however, is not for unbelievers but for believers. ²³So if the whole church comes together and everyone speaks in [foreign languages], and inquirers or unbelievers come in, will they not say that you are out of your mind? ²⁴But if an unbeliever or an inquirer comes in while everyone is prophesying, they are convicted [by all] and are brought under judgment by all ²⁵as the secrets of their hearts are laid bare. So they will fall down and worship God, exclaiming, "God is really among you!"

Key Observation. God is a God of order who expects his children to imitate him in that regard.

Understanding the Word. A few years ago, I spent a summer in Ethiopia teaching, preaching, and serving. Paul's words in 1 Corinthians 14:20–25 recall a sermon I gave. It was the first time I had preached with a translator. When preaching, I get in a rhythm but, for this, I had to slow down because he was translating my words into Amharic. I realized something mid-sermon: other than to the translator, my words mean nothing to those listening. I could have spoken five words in English or ten thousand; it did not matter. I was a foreigner speaking a foreign language.

My experience in Ethiopia helps me imagine what it might be like in a church full of multilingual people. If they were all speaking many languages at once, it would be chaos. Paul asks his hearers to consider the foreigners' perspectives. If they walked in and witnessed this, they would think everyone was out of their mind.

Imagine, however, a foreigner entering a congregation but witnessing a native Greek miraculously speaking in a foreign language. It would be a sign for that unbeliever: God is in this place and at work (14:22). In 1 Corinthians 14:21 Paul references Isaiah 28:11–12, which itself references Deuteronomy 28:49. In both contexts, God will use other languages and speakers of other languages for his purposes. In these verses, the term "the others," is often translated as "by foreign speakers." I render it "other-languaged speakers." Paul's point is this: God himself uses other languages for his ends. If God does this, it stands to reason that the strong in Corinth should too. They should have no resistance to other languages, especially if they fulfill God's work.

Thinking this way will stand as a mark of spiritual maturity. It will denote putting childish thinking behind becoming adults in the faith (14:21). Paul would no longer refer to those in Corinth as infants in Christ (3:1–2). Along with an openness to speaking other/foreign languages, Paul tells the assemblers to prophesy with care because it is a sign for believers. He says in 14:24–25 that if an unbeliever witnesses prophetic speech events, they would be convicted of their sin and recognize God's judgment against such sins. Then they would fall and worship him. Moreover, they would testify that God was among the worshipers there. The two gifts seem to have two different functions and audiences. Paul does not exalt one over the other. Both gifts can edify believers and unbelievers. Order and an openness to the Spirit are important factors. When used in an appropriate manner, God's gifts can unite his people and draw nonbelievers to him.

1. Why does it suggest about the nature of the church that it should be orderly and not chaotic? Is this meant to be reflected in the Christians' lives? How so?

2. Have you ever witnessed chaos in a church setting? What happened?

TWO
Three's Company

1 Corinthians 14:26–28 *What then shall we say, brothers and sisters? When you come together, each has a [psalm, a teaching,] a revelation, a [word in a foreign language or a translation]. Everything must be done so that the church may be built up. ²⁷If anyone speaks in a [foreign language], two—or at the most three—should speak, one at a time, and someone must [translate]. ²⁸If there is no [translator], the speaker should keep quiet in the church and speak to himself and to God.*

Key Observation. In Christianity, religion and relationship are not opposed to one another.

Understanding the Word. Ever heard someone say, "I am against organized religion"? The humor there is that the church is often disorganized! If it is *organization* folks are against, they should not have a hard time finding a church out of sorts. Some, however, place the emphasis on the *religion* part of the slogan. Their aim is to critique doctrine, hierarchy, and scandal. Some who self-identify as "Christian" share this sentiment. Many have copycatted this saying and put their own twist on it, saying, "It's not about religion, it's about relationship." A few years ago, a video went viral on the Internet with that claim. Many blindly jumped on the bandwagon.

Religion isn't inherently bad. Cicero argued that the word *religion* meant "to read." If we follow this, we might view Christianity as a practice of repeatedly returning to the Scripture to read, re-read, and read again. Christianity is a religion that focuses on nurturing relationships with God and others. Yet, it is wrong-headed to claim that Christianity is only about relationships. It is not. It is also not merely about religion. After all, James 1:27 says, at its best, Christianity is a pure and faultless religion.

While Paul talks about spiritual gifts and unity, speaking in foreign languages was on his mind (1 Corinthians 14:26–28). He will shift back to prophesying in 14:29–36. He reminds assemblers there is a necessary order to all this. Order is not a bad thing. Likewise, Paul using his apostolic authority to call for order, was not a bad thing. It was for the greater good of the community.

He begins by appealing to the congregants as his brothers and sisters (14:26). He is not switching to a new subject. He is singling out the subject to speak more about it. Later, he does the same concerning prophecy (14:29–36). He tells his siblings how they should operate when they "come together." Each believer has a spiritual gift and is worthy of inclusion in the gathering. Some may bring a hymn, a teaching, a revelation, a word in a foreign language, or a translation of that foreign word. There is space for each gift and for each person with a gift. No one gift is more important than another. No one person is more important than another. But each person must use their gift to edify the entire congregation.

In 14:27 Paul singles out two gifts: (1) speaking in a foreign language and (2) translating it. Then he offers guidelines for how to use these gifts. When the Spirit provides speakers with the ability to address foreigners in their language, everyone must listen. No one else may speak. When that person finishes, someone with the gift of translation must translate. This will edify everyone, not just a select few. Then, if the Spirit prompts someone else, they may speak. Similarly, someone must also translate.

Paul gives another rule: if no translator is present, the one with a word in a foreign language must remain silent (14:27–28). This person, regardless of their status and sex, must keep quiet. They may pray silently or speak within themselves, but they may not interrupt. Such guidelines create and maintain order in the assembly. Paul urges the worshipers, especially the strong, to no longer resist this gift.

1. Why is the modern slogan "Christianity is not about religion, it's about relationship" problematic?

2. How can having a healthy understanding of religion reflect positively on the Christian faith?

THREE
Submissive Misses or Missing the Point?

1 Corinthians 14:29–36 *Two or three prophets should speak, and the others should weigh carefully what is said. ³⁰And if a revelation comes to someone who is sitting down, the first speaker should stop. ³¹For you can all prophesy in turn so that everyone may be instructed and encouraged. ³²The [spiritual gifts] of prophets are subject to the control of prophets. ³³For God is not a God of disorder but of peace—as in all the congregations of the Lord's people.*

³⁴Women should remain silent in the churches. They are not allowed to speak, but must be in submission, as the law says. ³⁵If they want to inquire about something, they should ask their own husbands at home; for it is disgraceful for a [wife] to speak in the church.

³⁶Or did the word of God originate with you? Or are you the only people it has reached?

Key Observation. Both women and men are permitted to speak in church at any point as long as it is in an orderly manner.

Understanding the Word. First Corinthians 14:29–36 is difficult. In 14:34–36, Paul offers rules, quite like those concerning speaking in foreign languages, about prophesying. Only two or three should speak (14:29). Everyone else should listen and weigh carefully what the prophets say. Each should speak in turn, not simultaneously (14:31). The first speaker must allow others to speak and not hoard time (14:30). These guidelines fostered an atmosphere of mutual respect and edification.

In 14:32 Paul says, "The [spiritual gifts] of prophets are subject to the control of the prophets." This is not a reference to controlling the Holy Spirit, but prophets having control over themselves. Chaotic speaking is not the mark of a true prophet; rather, he/she could control his/her emotions and behaviors. Some ancient cults valued boisterous, ecstatic speech. There is no room for that in the church. Order is necessary (14:33). God is a God of order and peace. His people should imitate that.

The latter half of 14:33 goes with 14:34. Paul talks about silence. In 14:28 he teaches that, if anyone is about to speak in a foreign language and no translator is present, they should remain silent. In 14:30 he gives a similar example concerning prophesiers. In each instance, silence is linked to a specific activity. In 14:34–35 silence is linked to asking questions. Interruptive questioning is never listed as a spiritual gift. It is not sanctioned during worship gatherings because it can lead to disorder. Believers can bring psalms, prophecies, a teaching, etc., but not interruptive questions.

The NIV has, once again, mistranslated. Instead of using the word "wife/wives," which is correct, it uses "woman/women" (see also 1 Cor. 7:1–6 and 1 Cor. 11:2–16). In 4:17 and 7:17, Paul referred to the general law of keeping order in the churches. Such laws stem from Jesus's teachings and are rooted in both Scripture and Paul's opinion. There is absolutely no law against women speaking. The law in God's churches is this: no one interrupts others when they are exercising their gift(s) in worship. This is the norm Paul taught everywhere in all the churches (4:17; 7:17; 11:16; 14:33). Corinth did not have an orderly or norm-abiding structure in place. Paul urges them to set one up in 1 Corinthians 6. This would prevent interrogating one another during worship.

Note that Paul tells the wives they *should* speak in church via speaking/praying in foreign languages and prophesying (7:5; 11:5; 14:31). Wives/women were also permitted to speak with a psalm, teaching, revelation, or the translation of a foreign word. These verses do not silence women! They do not forbid women from evangelizing or preaching! What Paul does forbid is wives interrupting and interrogating their husbands (or others) during a worship service. Wives should ask their husbands questions at home rather than interrupting the gathering (14:35).

Ironically, Paul himself ends with two questions: "Or did the word of God originate with you? Or are you the only people it has reached?" The phrase "word of God" here does not refer to Scripture. It refers to the forms of speech previously mentioned, which originate with God and are spoken via humans. Interrupting, then, is an affront to God. It is an interruption of God's attempt to speak during worship. Practicing order does not arouse God's anger; rather, it honors him.

1. In your experience of worship have you ever seen the spontaneous use of a spiritual gift? If so, what happened? If not, what do you attribute that to?

2. How are the spiritual gifts Paul mentioned here complimentary (or meant to be, anyway)?

FOUR
Ifs, Ands, and Buts

1 Corinthians 14:37–40 *If anyone thinks they are a prophet or otherwise gifted by the Spirit, let them acknowledge that what I am writing to you is the Lord's command. ³⁸But if anyone ignores this, they will themselves be ignored.*

³⁹Therefore, my brothers and sisters, be eager to prophesy, and do not [refuse to speak in foreign languages.] ⁴⁰But everything should be done in a fitting and orderly way.

Key Observation. Our desire should not be to please others, but the Lord.

Understanding the Word. Recently, someone began pitching me ideas for marketing the church. Honestly, I felt gross just listening. Jesus does not desire PR campaigns. Nowhere do we find Paul, Peter, James, Augustine, Luther, Calvin, or Wesley advertising for Jesus. The way we live and serve should draw people to the church, not ads. Jesus does, however, desire that we be light to the world.

Behind every marketing campaign lurks a lust for relevance. Among Christians, zeal for relevance and novelty often leads to the first steps of heresy. Yet, the Christian faith is ancient. Believers hold fast to the teachings Paul received and handed on (1 Cor. 15:1–5). We cling to the teachings and commands of Jesus, which Paul himself refers to as "the law of Christ." Here in 1 Corinthians 14, at the climax of his discourse on using speech gifts, he says that what he has taught is the Lord's command (14:37). He uses similar terminology in 7:10 and 9:14.

There is no document, so far as we know, in which Jesus addresses prophesying or talking in foreign languages *in church*. Thus, Paul's appeal to Jesus may refer to a personal word he received from the Lord. In 14:29, as noted at the end of the preceding lesson, the apostle speaks about prophesying before others in the assembly. When someone offers a (personal-but-for-the-church) word from the Lord, everyone should weigh it carefully. Here, Paul is offering those in the congregation a word he received from the Lord. He calls them to weigh it with care. If anyone ignored this, they would be ignored (14:38).

The apostle's statement about being ignored referred to all he says in 1 Corinthians 14 in relation to receiving and sharing a word from the Lord. As he concludes this major section of his epistle, he tells all believers to be eager to prophesy (14:39). He also commands them again not to refuse to speak in foreign languages. These speech gifts are from the Holy Spirit and, when used properly, can edify the entire assembly (14:40). Abusing such gifts will bring about division and rejecting them is like trying to silence God and stifle his work and word.

Paul reminds us here that the Lord's commands are relevant to life and worship. We must be open to spiritual gifts and use them in a manner pleasing to God and edifying to the church. In 1:5 Paul mentions that God had bestowed spiritual gifts of knowledge and speech upon believers in

Corinth. Some, however, had abused those gifts and caused divisions. Here, in 1 Corinthians 14, the apostle provides guidelines to help prevent future fissures. If followed, these rules will nurture spiritual unity, which is relevant to pleasing God. Regardless of whether some consider such things outdated, we must hold fast to such teachings. Our desire should not be to please others, but the Lord. Once again, there are no ifs, ands, or buts about that.

1. What does it suggest about the church when it resorts to gimmicks and marketing ploys? How might non-believers find such actions distasteful?
2. Instead of adopting what seems socially relevant at the moment, what can the church do to draw people to it in honest and authentic ways?

FIVE
Hold on Tight

1 Corinthians 15:1–11 CEB *Brothers and sisters, I want to call your attention to the good news that I preached to you, which you also received and in which you stand. ²You are being saved through it if you hold on to the message I preached to you, unless somehow you believed it for nothing. ³I passed on to you as most important what I also received: Christ died for our sins in line with the scriptures, ⁴he was buried, and he rose on the third day in line with the scriptures. ⁵He appeared to Cephas, then to the Twelve, ⁶and then he appeared to more than five hundred brothers and sisters at once—most of them are still alive to this day, though some have died. ⁷Then he appeared to James, then to all the apostles, ⁸and last of all he appeared to me, as if I were born at the wrong time. ⁹I'm the least important of the apostles. I don't deserve to be called an apostle, because I harassed God's church. ¹⁰I am what I am by God's grace, and God's grace hasn't been for nothing. In fact, I have worked harder than all the others— that is, it wasn't me but the grace of God that is with me. ¹¹So then, whether you heard the message from me or them, this is what we preach and this is what you have believed.*

Key Observation. Salvation occurs in three tenses, not just one.

Understanding the Word. In 1 Corinthians 15:1–11 Paul uses the word "preached" as an *inclusio*—a literary device that functions like bookends on a shelf. It appears in 15:1 and 15:11. Everything in between (i.e., 15:2–10) concerns the content of Paul's preaching. In 15:1 he says believers in Corinth received what he preached ("the gospel" 15:2), and they took their stand upon it. *If*, and only *if*, they hold firm to the gospel, they will be saved.

This "if" statement is significant. It suggests that, after one trusts the gospel, one can also choose to stop trusting. Paul was not a once-saved-always-saved kind of guy. If someone pledges their allegiance but later reneges, they have committed treason, thereby rendering the former profession void. One must maintain one's allegiance in order to remain in a salvific state.

For Paul there are three tenses to salvation. First is the "past tense," the initial act of salvation (Eph. 2:8–9). Second is the "present tense," the ongoing process of salvation (2 Cor. 2:15; 3:11–15). Third is the "future tense," the culmination of salvation (1 Cor. 15:2; Rom. 8:22–23). The point is: a single profession in the past does not secure salvation. One's past pledge of allegiance must continue into the present. It will reach its culmination in the future. Salvation occurs in three tenses.

This raises the question: What is salvation? Salvation is deliverance from sin, death, and everlasting separation from God. Or, stated differently, salvation is the freedom to live in God's holy presence both now and in the future. This raises other questions too: How does one receive salvation? How is one delivered from sin and death? How is one given freedom to live in God's presence? Paul's response is to trust in or pledge one's allegiance to the gospel. He sums up the heart of the gospel in 15:3b–4: Christ died for our sins, was buried, and was raised on the third day. This statement, possibly an early creed, may have been difficult for some. Perhaps that is why Paul appeals to over five hundred witnesses (15:5–8). Some, like James, Peter, and Paul, pledged their allegiance to King Jesus and lost their lives because of it.

Throughout the letter, Paul discusses his authority as an apostle. While he uses strong terminology in 1 Corinthians 2, his remarks in 15:8–9 are quite harsh. He says he was the *last* apostle to see the risen Lord. It was, nevertheless, a mark of his apostleship. He says he was the *least* of the apostles because he had persecuted Christians. He says he was "the" (failed) apostolic *abortion*. What he means is that, of all the apostles, his call was the one many are most skeptical of. Many had doubted him and treated him with contempt. Many Jews of Paul's ilk would have viewed him as a turncoat. His own treated him with disdain, rejected him, and discarded him like an aborted fetus. But God had not discarded him.

In 15:10 he says he is, indeed, an apostle. God's grace continues to work in him. He says, "By God's grace I am what I am . . ." By God's grace he is an apostle. As an apostle, he preached the gospel. And, as children of Paul the apostle, those in Corinth trusted the gospel. Paul urges them to continue trusting (15:11). In that way, he finishes this section the same way he started, by talking about trusting the gospel he first preached to them.

1. What difference might it make in the life of a believer if they understand salvation in three tenses as opposed to a one-time event?
2. What does it suggest about the nature and character of God that he can use people like Paul, someone who possibly murdered Christians, to help advance the gospel?

WEEK ELEVEN

GATHERING DISCUSSION OUTLINE

A. **Open session in prayer.** Ask that God would astonish us anew with fresh insight from God's Word and transform us into the disciples that Jesus desires us to become.

B. **View video for this week's readings.**

C. **Ask:** What were key insights or takeaways that you gained from your reading during the week and from watching the video commentary? In particular, how did these help you to grow in your faith and understanding of Scripture this week? What parts of the Bible lesson or study raised questions for you?

D. **Discuss questions selected from the daily readings.**

   1. **KEY OBSERVATION:** God is a God of order who expects his children to imitate him in that regard.

      DISCUSSION QUESTION: Why does it suggest about the nature of the church that it should be orderly and not chaotic? Is this meant to be reflected in the Christians' lives? How so?

   2. **KEY OBSERVATION:** In Christianity, religion and relationship are not opposed to one another.

      DISCUSSION QUESTION: Why is the modern slogan "Christian is not about religion, it's about relationship" problematic?

3. **KEY OBSERVATION:** Both women and men are permitted to speak in church at any point as long as it is in an orderly manner.

   DISCUSSION QUESTION: How are the spiritual gifts Paul mentions here complimentary (or meant to be, anyway)?

4. **KEY OBSERVATION:** Our desire should not be to please others, but the Lord.

   DISCUSSION QUESTION: Instead of adopting what seems socially relevant at the moment, what can the church do to draw people to it in honest and authentic ways?

5. **KEY OBSERVATION:** Salvation occurs in three tenses, not just one.

   DISCUSSION QUESTION: What difference might it make in the life of a believer if they understand salvation in three tenses as opposed to a one-time event?

E. **As the study concludes, consider specific ways that this week's Bible lesson invites you to grow and calls you to change.** How do this week's scriptures call us to think differently? How do they challenge us to change in order to align ourselves with God's work in the world? What specific actions should we take to apply the insights of the lesson into our daily lives? What kind of person does our Bible lesson call us to become?

F. **Close session with prayer.** Emphasize God's ongoing work of transformation in our lives in preparation for loving mission and service in the world. Pray for absent class members as well as for persons whom we need to invite to join our study.

WEEK TWELVE

1 Corinthians 15:12–16:24

The Lord, the Apostles, and All the Brothers and Sisters in Christ

INTRODUCTION

As we approach the end of 1 Corinthians we may well find ourselves relieved. It takes vigor and perseverance to traverse the terrain of this epistle. Paul addresses tough topics: incest, prostitution, homosexuality, marriage, divorce, remarriage, idolatry, and other significant matters. First Corinthians gives us a glimpse into the lives of ancient believers. They had many things wrong. It was a bad look for the church. Yet, God did not forsake them. Still, Paul wants his siblings in Corinth to do better and be better.

In 1 Corinthians 15–16 Paul lists a handful of figures by name. While there are certain reasons for mentioning particular individuals, the plurality of names reminds us that "it takes a family." Paul entreats his siblings to look out for each other. He envisions everyone working together for the common good of all, which stems from a shared commitment to the gospel. At the heart of this gospel is the resurrection. Those who have pledged their allegiance to King Jesus must stand firm on the truth of the resurrection.

Just as Jesus was raised, they will also be raised. God has begun redeeming humans along with all creation. The resurrection reveals that God cares about humans, including their bodies. If God cares about human bodies, humans should too. We are to care for and treat our bodies with dignity and respect. The same is true of respecting others' bodies. The body is a holy temple and should not be mixed with what is vain. That is a form of blasphemy. Engaging in anything promoted by the sex industry, for instance, is a form of treasonous blasphemy. Such actions oppose the resurrection. Instead, we are to be a holy people just as our God is holy.

ONE
Dead or Alive

1 Corinthians 15:12–28 *But if it is preached that Christ has been raised from the dead, how can some of you say that there is no resurrection of the dead? [13]If there is no resurrection of the dead, then not even Christ has been raised. [14]And if Christ has not been raised, our preaching is useless and so is your [belief]. [15]More than that, we are then found to be false witnesses about God, for we have testified about God that he raised Christ from the dead. But he did not raise him if in fact the dead are not raised. [16]For if the dead are not raised, then Christ has not been raised either. [17]And if Christ has not been raised, your [belief] is futile; you are still in your sins. [18]Then those also who have fallen asleep in Christ are lost. [19]If only for this life we have hope in Christ, we are of all people most to be pitied.*

[20]But Christ has indeed been raised from the dead, the firstfruits of those who have fallen asleep. [21]For since death came through a man, the resurrection of the dead comes also through a man. [22]For as in Adam all die, so in Christ all will be made alive. [23]But each in turn: Christ, the firstfruits; then, when he comes, those who belong to him. [24]Then the end will come, when he hands over the kingdom to God the Father after he has destroyed all dominion, authority and power. [25]For he must reign until he has put all his enemies under his feet. [26]The last enemy to be destroyed is death. [27]For he "has put everything under his feet." Now when it says that "everything" has been put under him, it is clear that this does not include God himself, who put everything under Christ. [28]When he has done this, then the Son himself will be made subject to him who put everything under him, so that God may be all in all.

Key Observation. The resurrection is the basis of all Christian ethics.

Understanding the Word. When Paul wrote 1 Corinthians 15:12–28, part of his agenda was to get to the resurrection. For Paul, the resurrection was the basis of all Christian ethics; it should shape one's way of life. If one's view of the resurrection is off, one's manner of living likely will be too. That's precisely what was taking place in Corinth.

The previous fourteen chapters were building toward one point: a healthy understanding of the resurrection will make sense of all the problems in Corinth. Those involved in sexual improprieties, scandals with idol meat, and arguments over spiritual gifts must look to the resurrection. It provides the solution to such problems.

In 15:12–28 there are a plethora of references to resurrection. Paul also mentions death and dying. Death is the antithesis of resurrection. And that's the key to making sense of the resurrection as a solution to all the problems in the Corinthian assembly. All types of sin were present. The end result? Death. Resurrection is the antithesis of death. Resurrection defeats death. The resurrection means that those who have sinned can experience salvation. Sinners have earned death for themselves, but Christ's resurrection salvages them.

Christ's resurrection presupposes all believers' resurrections. Some in Corinth failed to realize that. Why? In 11:30, along with 15:6, 18, 20, and 51, Paul said some have "fallen asleep"—they have died. Yet, unlike Christ, who was raised only three days later, they were not. Some in Corinth seem to have misunderstood Paul's teaching on the resurrection. They may have expected a three-days-later resurrection for those who had died.

Or, perhaps they were thinking that, just as Christ had experienced resurrection soon after his death, all believers would too. When their expectations were not met, they grew skeptical. They might have started worrying about their own fates. Perhaps this is why Paul focuses so much on trust in 15:1–11. If someone ceases trusting, they also cease hoping. The hope of overcoming sin and the schisms it causes is lost. Committing such treason is a tantamount to a pitiable lie (15:13–17) and futile life (15:14, 17).

In 15:21–23 Paul mixes metaphors. He draws a contrast between Adam and Jesus (more on that in a future lesson) and refers to firstfruits. These were the first results of the harvest's produce given by priests as offerings to God (Ex. 23:16–19; 34:22–26; Lev. 2:12–14; 23:17–20; Num. 18:12–13; 28:26; Deut. 18:4; 26:2–10, etc.). They also functioned as a sign of a good harvest to come. When Paul describes Jesus, that's what he has in mind. Jesus's resurrection was a sign of the future resurrection of all believers.

Paul also draws on Psalm 110:1 (or 109:1 in the Septuagint), which is a royal psalm. It portrays the Lord ruling all. He additionally invokes

Psalm 8:1–9, a hymn that begins with a call to praise and then focuses on the majestic attributes of God such as dominion and power. Paul says all things, especially Jesus's enemies, will be under his feet. This may be a reference to Genesis 1:26–28. There, Adam received the command to rule over all. In 1 Corinthians 15:24–28, however, Jesus, the last Adam and culmination of all, is the ruler of all.

1. How does a correct understanding of Jesus's resurrection along with the promise of believers' resurrections have the ability put everything into perspective?
2. Why does misunderstanding the resurrection have the potential to lead to things like moral breakdown, relational division, and the destruction of the church?

TWO

The Walking Dead

1 Corinthians 15:29–34 NET *Otherwise, what will those do who are baptized for the dead? If the dead are not raised at all, then why are they baptized for them?* ³⁰*Why too are we in danger every hour?* ³¹*Every day I am in danger of death! This is as sure as my boasting in you, which I have in Christ Jesus our Lord.* ³²*If from a human point of view I fought with wild beasts at Ephesus, what did it benefit me? If the dead are not raised, let us eat and drink, for tomorrow we die.* ³³*Do not be deceived: "Bad company corrupts good morals."* ³⁴*Sober up as you should, and stop sinning! For some have no knowledge of God—I say this to your shame!*

Key Observation. There is a difference between figuratively dying to oneself daily and dying.

Understanding the Word. In 15:29 Paul continues talking about resurrection. He connects it to baptism, which was the source of numerous problems in the assembly (1:11–16). Recall: Paul baptized some in Corinth as did both Cephas (Peter) and Apollos. At baptism, some received spiritual gifts. Many believed that they would receive the same spiritual gifts as their baptizer. Thus, if Paul spoke in foreign languages and he baptized them, they would receive that same gift.

Arguments ensued, then, about which spiritual gifts were best and carried the most status. This also led to arguments about which apostle was best and carried the most status. Individuals appealed to their baptizing apostle to make themselves look good. Here Paul gets to the real heart of the matter (15:29–34). This raises a couple points.

First, note that in 1 Corinthians 15 Paul refers to the apostles several times. In 15:7–10 he says that the risen Lord appeared to all the apostles, including him. He then speaks about his call to be an apostle. Following this, he mentions his apostolic preaching, of which the centerpiece is Jesus's resurrection. His resurrection implies that, one day, God will raise all the faithful. Apostolic Christianity is resurrection-centered.

Second, Paul often describes himself and the other apostles as "the living dead." This occurs at least five times in 1–2 Corinthians (1 Cor. 4:9; 15:15–16; 2 Cor. 2:14–16; 4:10–11; 6:9). While Paul speaks frequently about dying daily and always facing death, he also mentions living for Christ as well as Christ living in him and the other apostles. Thus, and this is very important, *the apostles are the walking dead*. The apostles die to self every day for the sake of the gospel. This is what he is getting at in 1 Corinthians 15:29–32 when he comments about death and fighting beasts (persecutors; see Acts 19:1–41).

Third, in 1 Corinthians 15:29 Paul makes a contrast between "the dead" and "the actual dead." (The NIV completely misses this.) Paul's use of the word "actual" should not go unnoticed. Some are *actually* dead, while others are figuratively dead. He is differentiating between the apostles, "the walking dead" who are figuratively dead, and those in Corinth who have actually and recently died.

Taking these points together, we see that Paul is addressing here the very same issue he has talked about from the beginning. From the outset he deals with issues surrounding baptism by different apostles. Here, at the end, he continues addressing it. He simply refers to the apostles as "the dead," that is the figurative "walking dead," as opposed to "the actual dead." With that, he interrogates their flawed thinking about the apostles, baptism, and resurrection.

His logic is as follows: (1) the apostles believe in Jesus's resurrection and that they, too, will be raised; (2) if you are baptized by and on account of the apostles, and if you want to be like them, why do you misunderstand the resurrection?; (3) the apostles believe the resurrection and if you want to imitate them, you will, too; (4) if the apostles are wrong about the resurrection, they are pitiable liars. Why would you get baptized by and on account of pitiable liars?

Paul expects that his questions will force the Corinthians to rethink their beliefs and actions. In 15:32–34 he reveals how a flawed understanding of the resurrection, which is linked to baptism, is at the heart of the problems. Their corrupt views have led to a corrupt character and corrupt actions. For all their bickering and emphasis on the apostles, they are quite unlike them.

1. What does it mean to be one of Christ's walking/living dead? How does the Christian exhibit dying and living in everyday life?

2. When have you witnessed one of God's people truly exemplifying what it means to be one of the walking dead?

THREE
Resurrection

1 Corinthians 15:35–58 NET *But someone will say, "How are the dead raised? With what kind of body will they come?" ^{36}Fool! What you sow will not come to life unless it dies. ^{37}And what you sow is not the body that is to be, but a bare seed—perhaps of wheat or something else. ^{38}But God gives it a body just as he planned, and to each of the seeds a body of its own. ^{39}All flesh is not the same: People have one flesh, animals have another, birds and fish another. ^{40}And there are heavenly bodies and earthly bodies. The glory of the heavenly body is one sort and the earthly another. ^{41}There is one glory of the sun, and another glory of the moon and another glory of the stars, for star differs from star in glory.*

^{42}It is the same with the resurrection of the dead. What is sown is perishable, what is raised is imperishable. ^{43}It is sown in dishonor, it is raised in glory; it is sown in weakness, it is raised in power; ^{44}it is sown a natural body, it is raised a spiritual body. If there is a natural body, there is also a spiritual body. ^{45}So also it is written, "The first man, Adam, became a living person"; the last Adam became a life-giving spirit. ^{46}However, the spiritual did not come first, but the natural, and then the spiritual. ^{47}The first man is from the earth, made of dust; the second

man is from heaven. ⁴⁸Like the one made of dust, so too are those made of dust, and like the one from heaven, so too those who are heavenly. ⁴⁹And just as we have borne the image of the man of dust, let us also bear the image of the man of heaven.

⁵⁰Now this is what I am saying, brothers and sisters: Flesh and blood cannot inherit the kingdom of God, nor does the perishable inherit the imperishable. ⁵¹Listen, I will tell you a mystery: We will not all sleep, but we will all be changed— ⁵²in a moment, in the blinking of an eye, at the last trumpet. For the trumpet will sound, and the dead will be raised imperishable, and we will be changed. ⁵³For this perishable body must put on the imperishable, and this mortal body must put on immortality. ⁵⁴Now when this perishable puts on the imperishable, and this mortal puts on immortality, then the saying that is written will happen,

"Death has been swallowed up in victory."
⁵⁵"Where, O death, is your victory?
Where, O death, is your sting?"

⁵⁶The sting of death is sin, and the power of sin is the law. ⁵⁷But thanks be to God, who gives us the victory through our Lord Jesus Christ! ⁵⁸So then, dear brothers and sisters, be firm. Do not be moved! Always be outstanding in the work of the Lord, knowing that your labor is not in vain in the Lord.

Key Observation. Resurrection living includes looking after others, caring for God's planet, taking care of our bodies, and respecting others' bodies.

Understanding the Word. Quiz time. Do you remember what an *inclusio* is? If you said, "a literary device that functions like bookends," you're spot on. Just as the word "preach(ed)" in 15:1 formed an *inclusio* with 15:11, the concept of "standing firm" in 15:1 also forms an *inclusio* with being "steadfast" and "immovable" in 15:58. Christians are to stand firm on the gospel, which has resurrection as its centerpiece. Here, in 15:35–58, Paul discusses the who, what, when, where, why, and how of resurrection.

- 15:38: Who makes resurrection happen? *God.*
- 15:42, 51: Where does the old body go? *Nowhere, God transforms it.*
- 15:42: What happens when God transforms the body? *It becomes imperishable.*

- 15:49, 52: When does it happen? *At the return of Jesus.*

- 15:54: Why does it happen? *To show that God reigns and has defeated the law, sin, and death and has given believers everlasting life.*

- 15:38, 51, 57: How does it happen? *It's a mystery but, somehow, God does it.*

Paul employs several examples to illustrate his point: sun, moon, stars, seeds, wheat, fish, birds, and the first Adam. Believe it or not, Paul may have been borrowing from Aristotle who, centuries before, had written similar things. Aristotle thought that everything in existence had an opposite. The two opposites could never be the same. Moreover, one thing could not become its opposite.

For Aristotle, one animal could not become another. Earth could not become heaven nor the sun become the moon. Likewise, the dead could not become the living. It is this last one, however, where Paul breaks with Aristotle. He contends that the dead can live. Those who trust in Christ shall experience life after death. (Or, perhaps more appropriately, life after life.) At Christ's return, the physical body will assume a new, spiritual body. The perishable body will become imperishable. The one who took on a body like Adam will take on a new body like Christ. The old shall become new; the mortal shall become immortal (15:38–54).

At the resurrection everything—not just humans!—will change. Earth will experience transformation. This place, not some abode in the clouds, shall be the new heavens and new earth. Thus, part of the Christian life is accepting the invitation to usher in the resurrection here and now. It means looking after others, caring for God's planet, taking care of our bodies, and respecting others' bodies.

After the resurrection, neither death nor sin nor the (Mosaic) Law will exist (15:54–56). Christ's victory, however, will be on full display. Believers will bask in that victory (15:57). For now, the call is to stand firm, be immovable, and devote oneself to the Lord's work (15:1, 58). If one holds fast, neither one's trust in Jesus nor one's work will be in vain (15:32, 58). May our lives be an *inclusio* that resembles 1 Corinthians 15, one of steadfastness and standing firm on the gospel that has the resurrection at its center.

1. Have you ever found yourself in a circumstance where it was difficult to stand firm on your belief in the gospel and/or resurrection?

2. Why is it important to realize that the transformation of resurrection extends to all of God's creation, not only humans?

FOUR
Open-Door Policy

1 Corinthians 16:1–9 NABRE *Now in regard to the collection for the holy ones, you also should do as I ordered the churches of Galatia. ²On the first day of the week each of you should set aside and save whatever one can afford, so that collections will not be going on when I come. ³And when I arrive, I shall send those whom you have approved with letters of recommendation to take your gracious gift to Jerusalem. ⁴If it seems fitting that I should go also, they will go with me.*

⁵I shall come to you after I pass through Macedonia (for I am going to pass through Macedonia), ⁶and perhaps I shall stay or even spend the winter with you, so that you may send me on my way wherever I may go. ⁷For I do not wish to see you now just in passing, but I hope to spend some time with you, if the Lord permits. ⁸I shall stay in Ephesus until Pentecost, ⁹because a door has opened for me wide and productive for work, but there are many opponents.

Key Observation. Christians should allow the Holy Spirit to guide them in all areas of life, even down to travel and finances.

Understanding the Word. Many get nervous when preachers talk about money. I get it. There are too many stories of religious officials handling funds fraudulently. Such instances, along with "health and wealth" messages, create doubt. Some in Corinth doubted Paul. Money and itinerary, two of the main reasons he writes his follow-up letter, 2 Corinthians, are discussed here in 1 Corinthians 16:1–9. When Paul mentions the financial collection for the church at Jerusalem (16:1), the Corinthians know what he is talking about. It is the same collection referenced in 2 Corinthians 8:1–6, 9:1–4, and Romans 15:25–32. Paul promises to gather funds for the Jerusalem leaders during a famine (Gal. 2:1–10; cf. Acts 11:27–30).

This wasn't uncommon (Lev. 25:35–36; Deut. 15:1–18). Israel was commanded to look after its priestly class, the Levites, who had no land or cattle (Num. 18:23–24). Paul hopes that a financial gift from Gentile believers will create unity with their Jewish siblings in Christ. The apostle urges the Corinthians to contribute to the cause during worship gatherings (1 Corinthians 6:2). A little now will go a long way later. Paul will send the money, via several men from the congregation, to the church in Jerusalem (16:3). If it seems advisable, he will go too (16:4). Yet, he is willing to write letters of recommendation for the men approved to deliver the funds (16:3). An ancient document known as *P.Oxy.* 292 mentioned such letters. The following is my translation:

> (From) Theon. Greetings to the most honorable Tyrannus! Herakleides, the one giving this letter to you, is my brother. For this reason I strongly urge you to have him stay with you. Moreover, through a writing I even asked brother Hermias to inform you about him. You will be doing the greatest of things for me if you will acknowledge him. Above all, I pray for your health, freedom from injury, (and) good deeds. Goodbye.

Here the authority of the signatory is extended to the letter-carrier. If Paul did not travel with the men carrying the funds, a letter of recommendation would designate them as his stand-ins.

In 16:5 Paul transitions to his itinerary. He plans to visit Macedonia before arriving in Corinth. Currently, he is writing from Ephesus where a great door, despite many hardships, has opened for him to preach (16:8). Thus, when he arrives in Corinth, he plans to stay a while (16:6–7). Paul's travels were guided by the Spirit. He went where he was led. He did not go when a door closed (e.g., Acts 16:6). That's his policy. Eventually, Paul revisited Corinth. He conducted ministry there and spoke about money. Some may have grown even more skeptical, but others continued trusting and learning from him.

1. What does it suggest about the nature and character of the Spirit that the Spirit oversees Paul's apostolic travels and endeavors? And what does it suggest about Paul that he trusts the Spirit in this manner?

2. Has your experience in the church with money been positive or negative? Why?

FIVE
A Travelin' Band

1 Corinthians 16:10–24 NABRE *If Timothy comes, see that he is without fear in your company, for he is doing the work of the Lord just as I am. ¹¹Therefore, no one should disdain him. Rather, send him on his way in peace that he may come to me, for I am expecting him with the brothers. ¹²Now in regard to our brother Apollos, I urged him strongly to go to you with the brothers, but it was not at all his will that he go now. He will go when he has an opportunity.*

¹³Be on your guard, stand firm in the faith, be courageous, be strong. ¹⁴Your every act should be done with love.

¹⁵I urge you, brothers—you know that the household of Stephanas is the first-fruits of Achaia and that they have devoted themselves to the service of the holy ones—¹⁶be subordinate to such people and to everyone who works and toils with them. ¹⁷I rejoice in the arrival of Stephanas, Fortunatus, and Achaicus, because they made up for your absence, ¹⁸for they refreshed my spirit as well as yours. So give recognition to such people.

¹⁹The churches of Asia send you greetings. Aquila and Prisca together with the church at their house send you many greetings in the Lord. ²⁰All the brothers greet you. Greet one another with a holy kiss.

²¹I, Paul, write you this greeting in my own hand. ²²If anyone does not love the Lord, let him be [anathema]. Marana tha. ²³The grace of the Lord Jesus be with you. ²⁴My love to all of you in Christ Jesus.

Key Observation. All believers should be able to say amen to Paul's claims in 1 Corinthians.

Understanding the Word. Every Christian stands on the shoulders of others. We only know the gospel because our predecessors shared it with us. Christianity, by default, cannot be individualized. The church is a family. As Paul brings his letter to a close, he mentions numerous siblings in the faith. He speaks of his co-workers, Timothy (16:10–11) and Apollos (16:12–14). Stephanus, along with his household, who were the first converts in all of Asia (16:15–18) receive attention. Gaius, Achaicus, Priscilla, and Aquila are also on

Paul's radar (16:19–20). He tells those in Corinth how they should treat these siblings and one another.

Stephanus, Fortunatus, and Achaicus carried a letter to Paul in Ephesus from Corinth (see also 16:17). Paul says that they have refreshed his spirit. Because of their work, they deserved recognition (by him and the Corinthians). Priscilla and Aquila led the house church in Ephesus, just like Chloe did in Corinth (1:11). Stephanus may have also led a house church in Corinth (16:15). (While it is possible that Stephanus and Chloe were married and hosting one house church, one must ask why they are not mentioned together like Priscilla and Aquila.)

At the end of his letter, Paul tells the recipients to greet one another with a holy kiss, which was a common greeting in antiquity (Rom. 16:16; 2 Cor. 13:12; 1 Thess. 5:26; see also 1 Peter 5:14). This was not an erotic kiss, but a holy one. The apostle notes that he wrote the letter with/in his own hand. Whether or not someone had helped, this remark indicates that all the words are his. The letter is authentic. He makes similar comments in other epistles (Gal. 6:11; Col. 4:18; 2 Thess. 3:17; Phlm 19).

Next, Paul mentions loving the Lord right alongside anathema. The two cannot exist together. Either one hates the Lord or loves him. Paul uses this word in 12:3 to make the same point (see Gal. 1:8–9). This makes his remark in Romans 9:3 even more staggering. There he remarks that, if he could, he would trade his own salvation and become anathema so that his fellow Jews would be saved.

He ends the letter by extending grace to his hearers, which forms a nice *inclusio* to the entire letter. He sends his love and offers the valediction heard in ancient synagogues: "Amen!" It is an affirmation of all that has been said. That single word, "Amen," posed not only a challenge for the first hearers, but us too. Are we willing to stand with Paul and affirm everything said in this epistle? Many are not. My hope, however, is that you are. Amen!

1. When have you experienced an occasion where someone in the church deserved honor and recognition for their ministry?
2. What work of the Lord, whether in your own life and ministry or another's, have you recently said amen to?

WEEK TWELVE

GATHERING DISCUSSION OUTLINE

A. **Open session in prayer.** Ask that God would astonish us anew with fresh insight from God's Word and transform us into the disciples that Jesus desires us to become.

B. **View video for this week's readings.**

C. **Ask:** What were key insights or takeaways that you gained from your reading during the week and from watching the video commentary? In particular, how did these help you to grow in your faith and understanding of Scripture this week? What parts of the Bible lesson or study raised questions for you?

D. **Discuss questions selected from the daily readings.**

   1. **KEY OBSERVATION:** The resurrection is the basis of all Christian ethics.

      DISCUSSION QUESTION: How does a correct understanding of Jesus's resurrection along with the promise of believers' resurrections have the ability put everything into perspective?

   2. **KEY OBSERVATION:** There is a difference between figuratively dying to oneself daily and dying.

      DISCUSSION QUESTION: What does it mean to be one of Christ's walking/living dead? How does the Christian exhibit dying and living in everyday life?

3. **KEY OBSERVATION:** Resurrection living includes looking after others, caring for God's planet, taking care of our bodies, and respecting others' bodies.

   DISCUSSION QUESTION: Why is it important to realize that the transformation of resurrection extends to all of God's creation, not only humans?

4. **KEY OBSERVATION:** Christians should allow the Holy Spirit to guide them in all areas of life, even down to travel and finances.

   DISCUSSION QUESTION: Has your experience in the church with money been positive or negative? Why?

5. **KEY OBSERVATION:** All believers should be able to say amen to Paul's claims in 1 Corinthians.

   DISCUSSION QUESTION: What work of the Lord, whether in your own life and ministry or another's, have you recently said amen to?

E. **As the study concludes, consider specific ways that this week's Bible lesson invites you to grow and calls you to change.** How do this week's scriptures call us to think differently? How do they challenge us to change in order to align ourselves with God's work in the world? What specific actions should we take to apply the insights of the lesson into our daily lives? What kind of person does our Bible lesson call us to become?

F. **Close session with prayer.** Emphasize God's ongoing work of transformation in our lives in preparation for loving mission and service in the world. Pray for absent class members as well as for persons whom we need to invite to join our study.

Printed by Libri Plureos GmbH in Hamburg, Germany